Indian Women in Transition
A Bangalore Case Study

by

RHODA L. GOLDSTEIN

The Scarecrow Press, Inc.

Metuchen, N. J.   1972

Library of Congress Cataloging in Publication Data

Goldstein, Rhoda L
   Indian women in transition.

   Bibliography: p.
   1. Women in India--Case studies. 2. India--Social
conditions--1947-   I. Title.
HQ1743.G63   301.41'2'095487   72-4627
ISBN 0-8108-0527-8

To Bernard

CONTENTS

LIST OF TABLES

ACKNOWLEDGMENTS

A Fulbright-Hayes research fellowship enabled me to do the research upon which this book is based. The writing phase was assisted by a Rutgers University Research Council grant.

The then chairman of the Bangalore University Sociology Department, Sri. V. Muddalinganna, helped me in many ways--both intellectually and practically. I am also very much indebted to my main research assistant, Miss Leelavathi N., for her loyal, cheerful, and conscientious approach to her work. She participated in every aspect of the research procedure except for the completion of the analysis. Miss Maggie Matthews and Miss B. S. Ramamani also provided competent assistance at various stages. Miss Homaira Beghum, whom I met during the course of the pretest, proved to be an enduring friend upon whom I could count to share and analyze experiences.

The person who deserves most thanks is my husband and fellow sociologist, Bernard Goldstein. His critical judgment as well as support spurred me on to the completion of the book. My oldest daughter, Mary, took on many of the errands and tasks of the household, while my younger children, Meyer and Helena, were extremely cooperative.

Many of the people whom I met in India cannot be thanked by name, but I am grateful to them for their friendliness and willingness to share with me their thoughts about the subject of this book.

Chapter I

INTRODUCTION:
EDUCATED WOMEN IN A CHANGING SOCIETY

The interrelationships among women's education, their employment, and their family roles have received increased attention from scholars and popular writers in the last few years. Feminists have shattered long-held notions about "women's place" and the accepted myths about their nature and function. Much of the thrust in the United States has been directed toward the right of women to be employed outside the home, and toward freeing them from total preoccupation with child care. As American women have reexamined their place in their society they have found that, despite seeming progress, they still occupy positions that are inferior to men in every area of life--higher education, employment, politics, legal rights--and that economic rewards, power and status are distributed inequitably to them.

Perhaps most important, in terms of long-run consequences, are the attempts of American women to raise the level of their own consciousness about themselves and their roles. This involves thinking through and confronting a number of paradoxes and choices. At first glance it seems unlikely that women should accept, and be happy in, inferior positions--yet this is frequently the case. One is forced to examine the gains to be found in unquestioning acceptance of male dominance. Here the experience of every situation of superordination-subordination is instructive. The "good" inferior, who plays out his or her role deferentially, incurs the good will of the benevolent master. Treated as childlike, inferior, or helpless, he or she is the object of noblesse-oblige. Through artful manipulation, the inferior is able to get the most out of the system, whatever system it may be. The very servility or humility with which he approaches the master may be skillful pretense. And thus, in a way, the individual who does not have formal power achieves functional or informal power. The best exploration of this interrelationship, in the case of the female-male relationship, is to be found in Elizabeth Janeway's

Man's World, Women's Place.   She sums the point up in
this way:

> ... when women cling to their traditional role, it
> is not primarily because they find masochistic
> pleasure in being dominated (though no doubt some
> do) but because this role offers them power too:
> private power in return for public submission.
> This is the regular, orthodox bargain by which
> men run the world and allow women to rule in
> their own place [1 end of chapter].

These ideas are relevant to the present study.   The
formally subordinate role of Indian women to Indian men is
spelled out in sacred literature, in law, and in practice.
Yet there is no doubt that the woman who accepts this role
and plays it out to perfection, the ideal Indian wife and
mother, is revered and loved.   There is no doubt that many
or most Indian women do accept their traditional role of
dependence on male relatives.   But as the possibility of
economic independence, through respectable employment, becomes a reality for middle class Indian women, they may
be faced with new options.   If paid employment is the liberating factor that so many American feminists claim, then
is it liberating in every society and in every context?   What
other social changes flow from economic change?   Such
questions cannot be answered in simple or general terms.

However, one cannot question the fact that economic,
political and social developments have combined to create
innovations in the lives of a number of urban middle class
Indian women. [2]   The reformist movements of the last two
centuries, the current needs and aspirations of middle class
families, and the new opportunities for female education and
employment all interact to encourage change.   At the same
time, the probability exists that tradition, religious belief
and superstition still retain important influence on the lives
of women.

Part of this book will explore how the forces of tradition and modernity are or are not being reconciled.   It is
hoped to illuminate the route by which new conceptions of
women develop and become incorporated into or replace
older ones.   The book focuses on Indian women in transition, on the ways in which a group of young urban middle
class women (and their families) deal with their expanded
set of statuses.   How are the new roles engendered by

college education made to mesh with the traditionally family-centered female roles? What, if anything, are Indian women doing with their education? How do they view its effect on their lives? What problems do they encounter when they "take up" jobs? What jobs are available to them?

No one will deny that the old and the new continue to coexist in India. The question is how they coexist: whether there is conflict and turmoil in the lives of educated Indian women, or whether new practices are incorporated into traditional patterns. Gusfield explains the ideological acceptance of apparent behavioral change, as he delineates the misplaced polarity between tradition and modernity. [3] Bondurant makes the case that the potential for change is an essential element in Hindu philosophy, as one of the aspects of dharma. [4] And, indeed, India's vast body of religious and philosophical teachings has provided an ample source for social reformers who wished to validate 20th-century reforms by heralding back to traditions more liberal than those inspired by foreign domination.

Thus, might it not be that the modern woman, impelled by traditional notions of sacrifice and duty, will work in order to contribute to her family, rather than to satisfy her individual aspirations? But what if this role brings her into contact with beliefs and standards different from those of her family? What if it should make her susceptible to a "love" marriage? What if the ability to earn does create a more independent woman?

While the western social scientist may be surprised to find that tradition can be used to support new behavior patterns, he is unlikely to overlook the obvious potentialities for conflict. Given the unevenness of change, various role players will face inconsistent or conflicting expectations from others. The educated Indian woman, in contact with a broader culture than that of her home, learns about new role potentialities. The changes that college education brings about are varied and inconsistent; some women learn to live with these inconsistencies while others are in more open conflict. The educated women that are studied vary in their willingness to verbalize feelings of conflict. A few whose notions of women's rights and roles differ from those of their elders are openly prepared to rebel; many find little discrepancy between their new roles and their loyalties to old ones, while others who languish privately continue to accede outwardly to the wishes of their elders, as Indian women have usually done.

The initial research aim was quite simple: to learn
something about the roles of educated women in a changing
society. The research site was Bangalore, a South Indian
city of over one million inhabitants, which is the capital of
Mysore State and the seat of Bangalore University. [5]

Sri V. Muddalinganna, then chairman of the Sociology
Department at Bangalore University, directed my attention to
the increasing participation of women graduates in the work
force. The employment of middle class women appeared to
be a central consequence of the extension of higher education
It was decided to sample a group of graduates and post-
graduates who had finished their work for a degree fairly
recently. Questions were designed to get objective data
about education, employment and family background as well
as knowledge about how young women viewed the significance
of education in their lives. (See the Appendix for the specific questions.)

A 20 per cent sample was taken of women who had
graduated from Bangalore University in 1965, and who gave
Bangalore home addresses, a universe of 483. [6] Ninety-
nine women were selected for the sample, which included
graduates with bachelor's, master's, medical and law degrees. [7]

Preliminary discussions with members of the Sociolog
Department and women M. A. 's in sociology chosen as research assistants led to the formulation of a questionnaire,
which was pretested in September and October of 1966. The
revised questionnaire was then administered personally by
the research team, consisting of the author and three research assistants. Eighty-eight respondents, or 91 per cent
of the total, were interviewed in this manner, usually at
home but sometimes at the University or at work. Eleven
women were not living in Bangalore at the time of the contact, and eight responded to a mail questionnaire. This
phase of the work was completed in April 1967. However,
an additional member of the sample was located in Chicago,
Illinois and was subsequently interviewed by a female sociologist later in 1967. Thus, 97 cases are included.

The decision to use a questionnaire was based on
several considerations. Questionnaires are an accepted vehi
cle of social scientific inquiry in India. Suspicion could be

(and was) allayed by a printed schedule bearing the official sponsorship of the Bangalore University Sociology Department. Members of the sample, having been educated in the English medium in college, would be familiar with the language in its written form. The author could be confident that her American English, if difficult for some to understand, could be supplemented by the printed word. The instrument could be mailed to out-of-town respondents and mailed responses then provided a check on the clarity of wording.

Not knowing how the study would be received, there was no way of anticipating the completion of 97 questionnaires out of a sample of 99. The cordiality with which interviewers were received in Indian homes was striking, when compared with what one has come to expect from over-surveyed groups. Families frequently acted as if the visit was an "auspicious" occasion. The presence of the foreign scholar assured an interview in the few cases where a first contact by assistants had been met with suspicion. [8] But while the opportunity to participate in the interviewing process provided a fascinating introduction to Indian life for the foreign sociologist, the same questions may be raised about my role as about that of any other foreigner doing such research. For this reason, the research procedure will be described in some detail. The noted sociologist M. N. Srinivas has pointed out that there are disadvantages as well as advantages to having a culture studied by those native to it. [9] At the same time, the foreign field worker is enjoined to develop the necessary sensitivity to and empathy with the culture he or she is studying. Some of the research procedures which evolved were not typical of research done in the United States, but seemed suitable and natural in India. Among these were the practice of interviewing in teams of two, and of interviewing individuals in the presence of other family members.

Almost all of the interviews were administered by various combinations of two assistants, one a Brahmin and the other a Christian, and the author. [10] Another Brahmin assistant helped in the initial stages. The three assistants had been part of the same educational world as the young women being interviewed. Assistants were selected who could speak several languages and who would be able to conduct interviews in the respondents' mother tongue. In most cases this proved unnecessary. Many were fluent in the language and used it in informal contacts with friends as

well as in formal situations.   This was especially true of
Christian and Moslem respondents, not all of whom knew
Kannada, the main language of Mysore State.   One assistant's
fluency in Kannada and Tamil, and familiarity with Urdu, was
especially helpful in finding our way about the city and in
conversing with neighbors and older family members.

In the main, we adapted to the Indian convention that
females should not travel about the city alone.   However,
the Christian assistant was less bound by this tradition, and
she did some interviews by herself.   In later stages, the
author was also able to interview some respondents herself.
These interviews were set up in cases where the respondent
could be expected to be very fluent in English, and after a
certain amount of success had been experienced by the author
in the team interviews.

As Hanna Papanek points out, the foreign woman field
worker "not only has access to local women but can occupy
a surprisingly flexible position in local society."[11]   In addition to being free to travel about alone without censure, the
author was able to meet privately with Indian females.   I
was also regarded as somewhat distinct from other female
"elders" because of my unique status.   The assistants soon
became accustomed to a democratic approach and told others,
"She is like a friend."

When the other two assistants had left for permanent
posts elsewhere, Leela, the project mainstay, continued to
interview.   Her practice then was to take along a sister or
a friend for accompaniment; such assistance from female
friends and relatives was not considered an imposition.

In working together, the author and assistants acted
as a team, wordlessly deciding which of the partners was
to administer the interview schedule.   If the respondent was
fluent in English and seemed interested in talking to the
American, she was interviewed by the author.   An assistant
could and did conduct the interview if the respondent had
difficulty in understanding American English or preferred to
speak in Kannada.[12]   Twenty of the interviews were conducte
wholly or mostly in Kannada; the remainder in English.   This
procedure was developed as we assessed the reception of the
interview team.

An equal number of interviews were conducted in
privacy as in the presence of one or more family members--

almost 44 per cent of each. The remaining 13 per cent took place in the company of a friend of the respondent. The presence of sisters or girl friends during the interviews seemed to make the respondents more comfortable, gayer, and more informal. Given a culture in which young women are often accompanied by their friends, the group situation was a very natural one. In cases where a parent was present in the room, one member of the interview team was usually able to engage him or her in a separate conversation. Occasionally a young woman would fill out the questionnaire herself while we talked to the parents. This enabled her to express private views which might be at variance with those of family members. Despite the obvious disadvantages, the group situations made it possible for us to converse with more family members informally than would have occurred otherwise.

Assistants were instructed to write down their comments after leaving the interview situation. All quotations from interviews and additional conversations are offered in the original to provide an authentic and immediate flavor of the tone and style of the interviewers' impressions and the interviewee's responses. They seem, in many ways, to be attitudinally revealing. The remarks of assistants, which will be quoted from time to time, proved very instructive as examples of peer group judgment. For instance, the most extremely reticent respondent, who depended on her father for assistance throughout the interview, was described in the following way by an assistant:

> The girl has no individuality whatsoever. For everything she was depending on her father's reply.... She was very shy.... I was quite surprised to know that a graduate is unable to answer a simple question like at what age a girl should get married.... The interview wasn't very impressive but it is interesting to know that there are such types of girls in spite of education [Research Assistant A, about interview 106].

An initial obstacle was that of locating the desired respondent. Addresses had to be culled from various university lists. The assistants were unfamiliar with many Bangalore neighborhoods, and street addresses had been changed twice during the previous few years. Starting our interviews in areas familiar to the assistants provided the needed confidence to explore more difficult locations. Much

use was made of informal contacts to find women who had
married or moved for other reasons. The Moslem respondent referred to earlier in a footnote was located through inquiries among neighbors in the vicinity of her parents' former home.

In almost all cases, locating an address resulted in
the ultimate granting of an interview. If no one was at
home, we left a card making an appointment for our return.
The research assistants utilized the convention of selecting
a time and date for our future appointment, in the expectation that the individual would try to be at home when we returned. Through knowledge of the working schedules of government offices and schools we could choose times appropriate for working respondents. [13]

Assured the hospitality of Indian homes, how could
we judge the honesty of responses? Both objective and sub-
jective observations helped. The home and style of life of
a respondent could be noted, as well as her identification of
the family's class position. Cultural conventions about the
kinds of information one makes public were revealed in the
ease and rapidity, or reticence, with which certain answers
were given. For example, data about the education of family
members tended to be presented with great specificity. In-
formants occasionally mentioned that age or family income
had been represented differently for official purposes, such
as gaining scholarships. Naming one's salary fairly accurately seemed to be standard procedure for members of the
sample. The opinions of family members on various issues
were described with no hesitation. However, questions
which sought the young woman's own opinion did cause some
difficulty. For example, a number of women professed that
they had not thought about their own future marriages. In
Chapter IV an analysis is made of this particular response,
which turned out to be the conventionally modest one. In
some cases the conventional response was not given, leading
us to formulate a hypothesis about the deviant cases. [14]
Many respondents volunteered information about the arranged
marriage system and the fact that it was not appropriate for
them to think about marriage. However, they were quite
willing to discuss the marriages of friends or other family
members. It was here that some respondents would talk
about the anxiety of women (never themselves) to get married

A range in willingness to express independent thinking
was observed. Some women were highly articulate and philo-

sophical; others gave brief answers and appeared to be reticent to state their individual opinions. Perhaps the most difficult thing for the researcher to ascertain, in such a situation, is whether the individual is following convention or truly has no independent opinion on the matter at hand. Margaret Cormack's assertion that the Hindu woman's strong identification with family inhibits her sense of individuality is evident in some cases. [15]

Rama Mehta, in her recent study of 50 highly educated Indian women, suggests that there are areas in which Indian women accept the right of parents to make decisions for them. She states, "They had been brought up to leave important decisions to their parents. They were not reared to take responsibility for their actions and the right of their parents to marry them was part of their whole upbringing. "[16] However, a related aspect of her training makes the Indian woman unwilling to express disagreement with her parents when she does have an independent opinion. Many answers also reflect a reliance on fate or an expectation that fate will determine one's future. Thus, even when encouraged, some respondents appear to be unable or unwilling to look into the future. They find it difficult to respond to a question which asks what they would like to do in the next few years if given free choice. Varying degrees of fatalism are also expressed in answers about marriage.

An indication of change is the fact that some respondents openly expressed disagreement with their parents. In contrast to Cormack's generalization, there are new types of women emerging who take a more active stance toward their fate and who assert individuality.

The 1966 report of the Indian Education Commission (the D. S. Kothari Report) has shown that more and more Indian women are going on not only for college education but also for post-graduate studies. [17] These highly educated women, particularly those who remain in urban areas, are the ones most likely to be affected by currents of change and to reflect modifications in female roles. Can generalizations be drawn from the data to educated women in other parts of India? The answer must be conditional. Where similar events or circumstances affect women throughout the country, similarities in response may be expected. For example, legislation redefining such matters as women's property rights or age of marriage will apply to the whole country and change the fate of many women. New occupational oppor-

tunities will draw to them women from many different castes
or communities.

Certain changes will be most dramatic in the big cities, but an interchange of persons between cities and village
takes place.   Bangalore's special characteristics as a south-
ern city having a heterogeneous population, as a former sea
of the British, as an educational center, as a city to which
industrialization came later than that of other major cities--
will affect its rate of change.   Bangalore women tend to be
more conservative than those in Bombay yet more subject to
change than those in smaller south Indian cities, and certain
ly far different from those in villages.   Yet, as 19 per cent
of India's population is now urban, we can expect the city,
as a center of change, to have eventual influence on the village.

At the same time it must be remembered that college
educated women are a tiny group, and that although there is
a lessening gap between the educational level of men and of
women, the percentage of Indians with college degrees remains extremely small.   According to the Indian Ministry of
Education, 0. 7 per cent of females and 2. 8 per cent of male
in the corresponding age groups were enrolled in undergradu
ate (arts, science, and commerce) colleges in 1960-61.   On
per cent of males and 0. 1 per cent of females were enrolled
in professional undergraduate education; while 0. 5 per cent
of males and 0. 1 per cent of females were in general and
professional post-graduate studies at that time.   These figures include both urban and rural India. [18]

Notes

1.   Elizabeth Janeway, Man's World, Women's Place (New
     York: Morrow, 1971), p. 56.

2.   This point is made also by Amarjit Mahajan, "Women's
     Two Roles: A Study of Role Conflicts, " Indian
     Journal of Social Work 26 (January 1966):   377-380.

3.   Joseph Gusfield, "Tradition and Modernity: Misplaced
     Polarities in the Study of Social Change, " American
     Journal of Sociology 72 (January 1967):   351-362.
     Among the points made by Gusfield is that tradition
     and modernity may be mutually reinforcing rather
     than systems in conflict (p. 356).

4. Joan Bondurant, "Traditional Polity and the Dynamics of Change in India," Human Organization 22 (Spring 1953): 5-10.

5. Bangalore was the site of Aileen Ross' The Hindu Family in its Urban Setting (Toronto: University of Toronto Press, 1961) and her Student Unrest in India (Montreal: McGill-Queen's University Press, 1969).

6. All accredited colleges in Bangalore are affiliated with and their students graduate through Bangalore University. The universe included more than five-sixths of all women receiving degrees that year. Graduates and post-graduates were chosen roughly proportionate to the total number of women receiving the various degrees in 1965. Twenty-eight respondents held degrees higher than the simple B. A. or B. Sc. Since the degree partially determines one's occupational field, the manner of selection affects the distribution of respondents found in various occupations. Because a weighted sample was used, the type of degrees held and occupational status of respondents represent the universe.

7. Of the original names and addresses selected, four could not be found and were replaced on a random basis. There were no refusals.

8. Interviews were rated according to the degree of cooperation received. Only two respondents were rated quite reticent or uncooperative, and another 13 per cent somewhat reticent. The average degree of cooperation was one in which the respondent willingly agreed to be interviewed at the time we chose, answered all questions, almost always offered us some refreshments, and chatted with us about other things. We rated as exceptionally friendly those who wanted us to return, who prepared elaborate food for us, who promised to visit the author, or who wanted me to meet other family members not present at the time. We rated almost one-third as exceptionally friendly. In one case a Moslem woman and her husband called at my home to deliver her mail questionnaire, which she had received while visiting her parents in Pakistan.

9. M. N. Srinivas, Social Change in Modern India (Berke-
    ley: University of California Press, 1966), pp. 147-
    163.

10. Miss Leelavathi N. was present at 75 per cent of the
    interviews, the author at 63 per cent. (The initial
    "N" stands for Nagappa, the name of Leela's father,
    but it is not customary for her to use the full name.

11. Hanna Papanek, "The Woman Field Worker in a Purdah
    Society, " Human Organization 23 (Summer 1964):
    160.

12. Rama Mehta indicates that her in-depth interviews with
    educated women from various Indian provinces were
    all conducted in English. See The Western Educated
    Hindu Woman (New York: Asia Publishing Company,
    1970.)

13. In only one-third of the cases did we find the respond-
    ent at home and conduct the interview on the first
    visit. The median number of contacts required was
    two but sometimes three or more were needed.
    Persistence is taken seriously in India, and the de-
    termined individual tends to get his way. Thus, a
    post-card follow up to a mail questionnaire often led
    to results. It signified that we were eager to have
    the questionnaire filled out. Some respondents apolo
    gized for the trouble entailed in reaching them.

14. A number of women volunteered out of context that they
    themselves did not plan to marry, thus taking an ac-
    tive position rather than a fatalistic one.

15. While Cormack feels that individualism will have an im
    pact on the "group-mindedness" of Hindu women she
    maintains that the traditional values of interdepend-
    ence and harmony will persist and condition the de-
    velopment of the individuality of Hindu women [op.
    cit. , p. 193]. About this one assistant said, "The
    submissiveness and resignation in Hindu women
    which the author discusses is merely superficial.
    Education has taught the woman the ideas of initia-
    tive, equality, individualism and competition. "

16. Mehta, op. cit. , p. 112.

17. Report of the Education Commission, (1964-66), Education and National Development (New Delhi: Government of India Press, 1966), p. 300. According to the report, the number of girls enrolled in undergraduate courses in arts, commerce, and science for every 100 boys increased from 13 to 24 between the years 1950-51 and 1965-66. At the post-graduate level, the increase was even slightly more favorable. Hidden in these statistics is the fact that girls are poorly represented in engineering, medicine, and commerce--the most preferred fields for men.

18. Ibid. p. 100, Table 5.5. In Mysore State, only 22 persons per 10,000 were currently enrolled in higher education (p. 126, Table 6.6).

Chapter II

SOCIAL AND ECONOMIC CHARACTERISTICS OF THE BANGALORE SAMPLE

Susheela is known to one of our research assistants by reputation as an exceptionally beautiful and talented young Brahmin. She turns out to be of rather fair complexion (for South India), with large regular features, excellent diction, and great poise. Having overcome her widowed mother's objections to higher education she is now studying for a master's degree in English. Susheela lives with her mother and two elder unmarried sisters in a rather new but increasingly crowded residential area. Their house occupies its own plot among a row of similar small houses, none of which has a compound worthy of the name. Most do have a wall or fence surrounding their small piece of garden, and an entrance gate. This privacy of entry marks them as part of the middle class. Susheela greets us most cordially at the door and invites us into a small front room. Evidence of established middle class style is seen again in many tasteful decorative arrangements and wall hangings. The home is furnished with chairs and sofas, and we move into a second large room, definitely a mark of relative comfort. (Many homes we visit have but one small front room in which to entertain visitors.) Susheela's father, now deceased, was a "superintendent," though it is not clear of what. His education, as well as her mother's, is that of a matriculate. Family income is described as between 500 and 799 rupees monthly and the young woman considers herself middle class. This designation is given in spite of the fact that her mother speaks English well and that Susheela pilots her own motor scooter to and from the university. Style of life might suggest upper-middle class status were it not for the family's income.

Farzana is a 24-year-old Moslem who has her master's degree in sociology, and is now teaching in a Methodist high school. Her address is one which our Hindu assistant cannot fathom. With the aid of a Moslem acquaintance (who herself lives in another part of Bangalore) we are able to locate the street in the congested and dirty Cantonment market

ket area. [2]   Inquiring at various shops we are directed to
one where Farzana's father is working as a job typist.   He
turns out to be a military pensioner who cordially offers to
take us to his home.   As we encounter a neighborhood boy,
however, Farzana's father turns the errand over to him and
returns to work.   The house is not far from the shop, a
nondescript stone dwelling attached to others in a row, and
fronting on the street.   Neighborhood women gather around,
explaining to us in Urdu that the girl's mother is dead and
that the girl is a teacher and will be home on a particular
day.   These somewhat shabbily arrayed neighbors share the
same house and each other's business, a characteristic
seemingly more true of the less affluent because of their
close contiguity.

Upon our return visit, we again meet Farzana's father, who apologizes for what he calls "our poor standard of
living."   Passing the cage of chickens in the hallway, we
enter a very small neat apartment of two or three rooms
which has been brightened up by cheerful matching of curtains
and pillow cushions.   Farzana indicates that her father has
a B.A. degree and was a lieutenant prior to being retired
because of injuries.   Her mother had finished middle-
school. [3]   Farzana has one brother and one sister, lists
family income as between 300 and 499 rupees per month and
she, too, calls herself middle-class.

Mary Sheela, a 22-year-old Christian B.A., seems
similar to Farzana in economic circumstances.   She is a
clerk in the state government purchasing department and her
father is a retired military mess manager, his education
being "intermediate."[4]   The mother, employed as a com-
pounder of medicine in a hospital, has finished her "Senior
Cambridge."   Mary Sheela has one sister, now married and
living away from home.   Our assistants found this house
after difficulty, as it is set in from an alley which is off
the main road.   The land around it is low and damp, and
animals roam in front of the door.   A neighbor's child wan-
ders in and out at will.   We visit in the one main room,
which appears to serve many purposes, and see a small
kitchen further inside.   Mary Sheela lets us know that she
is helping to support the family, whose income is between
300 and 499 rupees per month, and she lists herself as middle-class.

Indira is a married 23-year-old Brahmin B.A. who
has come back to her mother's home for the delivery of her

first child.   The mother and two younger sisters occupy a
second-floor flat which is small but neat and tastefully furnished, in a Hindu residential area.   The interview is held
in the main room but we also get a chance to peek at the
new baby swinging in a wooden cradle, in a small nearby
room.   Indira's father, now deceased, was an accountant
who held a Bachelor of Commerce degree and a banking
certificate.   The mother's education is intermediate and she
speaks excellent English.   Indira lives in Bombay, in an
independent household, with her engineer husband.   She
states that their income is between 500 and 799 rupees per
month, and checks upper class to identify her status.   Our
assistant comments on this in her notes, as follows: "She
has written that she belongs to the upper class but this
house was very modest.   I can't decide anything because she
lives with her husband. "   My own comment on this house, in
comparison with others seen during the interviews, is "aver
age. "

Monica is a wealthy young Sindhi woman, age 22, who
describes family income as well above 800 rupees per month
the point above which we did not ask for specific figures.
Her house is large, and extremely well-furnished.   Like a
few other homes that we visit it has a telephone, the mark
of affluence in Bangalore.   The area is a quiet one, but not
new, and does not have the large compounds characteristic
of some other areas.   Monica has three brothers and five
sisters, two of the latter living at home.   The other sisters
are living with their husbands, while one sister-in-law has
been added to this household.   Monica's father, the proprietor of a silk factory, has an intermediate education, while
her mother lacks even a primary school education.   Monica
has not been allowed to continue past her bachelor's degree,
for fear that she will expect a very highly educated mate.
Her father is evidently seeking a bridegroom for her, but
some candidates, otherwise promising, have not had auspicious horoscopes, which has caused delay.   Monica would
like to work but is not allowed to, and spends her days attending her ailing mother.   She lists her class as upper
middle.

Perhaps the most affluent home encountered was one
that we did not get to enter.   It is the family home of a
young woman now residing in the United States with her engineer husband, who is working for an American firm.   Mo
hini responded to a mail questionnaire after we were fortunate enough to obtain her address from a family member.

Her parents' home is in a very wealthy section where Europeans prefer to reside and like others in the area, their luxurious compound is encircled by a high stone wall. Mohini's father is also an engineer and her mother is a college graduate. Family income is described as above 800 rupees per month, and Mohini is one of the four respondents calling herself upper class. While her name is of Sindhi origin, she writes only that she is Hindu and lists no caste designation.

These are impressionistic recollections of the varied homes and young women we encountered. Almost three-quarters of the interviews took place in homes--either those of the individual's parents or guardians, those of her in-laws, or her own nuclear household--affording ample opportunity to observe the range in dwelling places. Let us consider more systematically now some of the important background and family characteristics of the sample.

As indicated in Table 1, the respondents are mostly single. Three-quarters of them are Hindu, 15 per cent are Christian, and 9 per cent are Moslem. [5] The median age of both single and married respondents is 22. At the time of the study, 44 per cent are employed, almost one-third are studying for advanced degrees, and about a quarter are neither working nor in school. [6] Subtracting the number of young women who are seeking employment from this last group, we find that less than 15 per cent of the sample will probably not enter the labor force. While those now studying may increase this percentage somewhat, our data strongly points to the supposition that acquisition of advanced degrees will lead to employment.

The predominance of three major caste groupings in South India has been noted elsewhere, although nomenclature varies. [7] Theoretical disagreements regarding the most appropriate terminology to use in classifying India's hierarchical groups need not be of concern here (see, for example, Ghurye and Mandelbaum[8]). First, caste is not used as a major variable. Secondly, each respondent has no difficulty in naming her "community" or jati, the caste or sub-caste of which she considers herself a part. This community is an endogamous grouping, determined by birth, which serves as a source of identification for the individual and as a means of placement in the prestige hierarchy of such groups in South India.

TABLE 1: GENERAL CHARACTERISTICS OF THE BANGALORE SAMPLE

	Number	Percent of Total*
Marital Status		
Single	78	80
Married	19	20
Religion		
Hindu	73	75

Caste or community of Hindu	Number	Percent of Hindu
Brahmin	51	70
Non-Brahmin	18	25
Scheduled Castes	2	2
Other	2	2
Total	73	99

	Number	Percent of Total*
Christian	15	15
Moslem	9	9
Present status		
Now employed	43	44
Studying for advanced degree	29	30
Neither employed nor in school	23	24
Doing unpaid religious work	2	2
Age		
Median of sample	22	
Mode of sample	21	
Median of married respondents	22	
Mode of married respondents	22	

*Percentages in this and succeeding tables may not total 100 per cent, as figures are rounded. N = 97

Brahmins are the only group that describe themselves by both caste and sub-caste names, such as Sarasweat Brahmin. They constitute about half of the sample and 70 per cent of the Hindus. Most of those who are not Brahmins name their communities by one term, such as Bhandari, Nair, or Reddy, and not in terms of the four traditional Varnas. [9] Eighteen separate communities are among these, and none is represented more than twice. One individual identifies herself as a Kshatriya and one as a Vaishya. All of these are classified here as non-Brahmins, and they constitute 19 per cent of all respondents, or one-quarter of the Hindus. Two women are Sindhis and are classified in Table 1 as "other," since they do not give specific caste names. The third major caste grouping of South India, the Scheduled Castes, or Harijans, are represented by only two individuals, or 2 per cent of the sample. This percentage is interesting in light of the claim that compensatory legislation aiding "backward classes" has bordered on discrimination against Brahmins in Mysore State. [10]

While a few tables will provide some comparisons between Brahmins and other castes, it is obvious that most castes are not represented in numbers that would be significant for quantitative analysis.

One must agree with Rosen that "any attempt to define the middle class [in India] can easily become a morass." [11] However, while we need not go into the many complexities of class definitions, it is important to show that most respondents are accurately classified as middle class. This is necessary because class status enters into our analysis in a crucial way.

Data on income, own identification of class, education and occupation of parents, and type of dwelling quarters can be measured against the criteria of class presented by various authors.

Misra lists a wide range of occupational groups comprising the Indian middle classes, excluding from these all types of manual workers and also teachers below "the upper range" of secondary school teachers. Only the highest range of government or business officials is considered to be above middle class. Misra also includes as part of the middle classes, "the main body of full-time students engaged in higher education at a university or comparable level." [12] If we accept this criteria, then our respondents, all college

graduates, are members of the middle class by definition.
What about their parents?

Rosen defines the urban middle class in terms of
three groups, describing the type of occupational groups that
fall into each strata as follows:

> On a top level, it is clear that the leading business
> men in India, the leading members of the govern-
> ment bureaucracy, and the leading intellectuals
> should be included. The higher income profession-
> als, scientists and technicians, the professional
> managers in industry, and the large merchants
> should also be associated with the upper group
> within the middle class. Below these are the
> mass of clerks and relatively minor officials in
> government offices and private commercial and
> industrial firms, the school teachers, working
> journalists, struggling professionals and the petty
> shopkeepers and possibly small-scale industrialists.
> Although this lower middle-class group generally
> has a high rate of literacy and education and an
> inclination toward white-collar jobs, individual in-
> comes are low. [13]

Note that Rosen does not distinguish an upper class from the
upper range of the middle class.

The fathers of our respondents are engaged in a variety of occupations but, taking the largest possible estimate,
not more than 9 per cent could be classified as lower or
working class (see Table 2). Several hold permanent though
low-paid government positions; the acquisition of higher education by their children probably indicates upward mobility.

There is no clear way of distinguishing, on the basis
of occupation, between the very small elite upper class that
some writers recognize and the upper level of the middle
class. A man listed as "proprietor" may own a thriving
business or a modest one. In the case of fathers described
as "officials" the importance of their positions cannot be
readily determined.

Middle-class mothers are not likely to have worked
outside the home except in a very few types of jobs. Teach
ing and medicine are the most acceptable occupations for
Indian women, and it is here that we find most of the

TABLE 2: FATHERS' OCCUPATIONS

	Number	Per Cent
Professional and managerial TOTAL	69	70
Proprietor or landlord	14	14
Manager, supervisor or official	29	30
Doctor, lawyer or engineer	14	14
College teacher	4	4
Other professional	8	8
Semi-professional and white-collar TOTAL	19	20
School teacher	2	2
Semi-professional or technical	8	8
Clerical or white collar	9	9
Working class TOTAL	9	9
Armed forces or police	4	4
Skilled worker or operative	2	2
Not given or not clear[a]	3	3
TOTAL	97	98[b]

a. This table is intended to give highest possible estimate of working class families.

b. Totals and sub-totals calculated separately and rounded.

mothers who have worked. [14] Of 11 mothers who are not, or
were not, primarily housewives, three are physicians, one
is a college teacher, five are school teachers, one does
pharmaceutical work, and the last held a job in public trans
portation prior to her death. The two nonprofessional positions are held by Christians, among whom traditional norms
against work are probably not as strong. In all, then, not
more than 11 per cent of mothers have worked outside the
home, and most in "respectable" middle-class occupations.

Considering income as a criterion of class, Rosen di
vides the Indian middle class into three income groups: the
upper-middle class, which receives incomes above Rs. [ru-
pees] 12, 500 per year, the middle-middle class with income
from Rs. 3, 600 to 12, 500 per year, and the lower-middle
class with incomes below Rs. 3, 600 per year. He maintai
that during the decade 1951-1961, the number in the lower
middle class "defined as white collar employees with incomes below Rs. 300 per month" increased by over 100 pe
cent. Thus the representation of people in the lowest stratu
of the middle class can be expected to be quite large. According to Rosen,

> A recent survey of the incomes of middle-class
> families in the four major cities of India--Calcutt
> Bombay, Delhi, and Madras--shows that in 1958-
> 59 the average monthly income of all families
> ranged from about Rs. 300 to about Rs. 380 per
> month, of which Calcutta had the highest average
> and Madras the lowest. About 60 per cent of the
> families had incomes below the average of Rs.
> 300 per month, with the maximum concentration
> in the range of Rs. 100 - 200 per month. [15]

These income figures may be used for rough compa
son with the income figures given by members of our samp
in 1966-67.

As can be seen in Table 3, less than one-tenth of
those studied report family income to be below 300 rupees
per month, and almost three-fifths say it is between 300
and 799--putting them in the middle of the middle class ac
cording to Rosen's divisions. About one-third have family
incomes of 800 rupees or more per month, a figure which
Indian academic colleagues considered a rather comfortable
income but which falls partly into Rosen's middle segment
of the middle class. While a few respondents with high

TABLE 3: CLASS IDENTIFICATION BY FAMILY INCOME

Family Income in Rupees per Month	Class Identification									
	Total		Upper		Upper Middle		Middle		Lower Middle	
	No.	%	No.	%	No.	%	No.	%	No.	%
Below 299	7	7	0	0	0	0	7	11	0	0
300 - 499	25	26	0	0	2	7	22	34	1	1
500 - 799	33	34	1	25	9	32	23	36	0	0
Above 800	32	33	3	75	17	61	12	19	0	0
Total	97	100	4	100	28	100	64	100	1	100
	100%		4%		29%		66%		1%	

incomes may belong within the tiny elite upper class, less
than a tenth of those in the highest income bracket so classify themselves. If we combine income with our evaluation
of class position, only 3 per cent fall within the upper clas
(see Table 3).

Two criteria of class, father's job and family incom
are related. The median income of those holding professio
al and managerial jobs is between Rs. 500 and 799; of thos
holding middle and lower level jobs, between Rs. 300 and
499 monthly.

The fathers of somewhat less than two-thirds of the
sample are working. Three who are retired from their
regular occupations and who have taken other jobs are included among the employed, but 16 per cent are retired an
not working. [16] More than a fifth of the fathers, as contrasted with 8 per cent of the mothers, are deceased. Thu
due to death and retirement, more than one-third of the
families are deprived of the regular income of a father.

Respondents were asked, "What class do you consid
your family to be?" and given a choice of upper class, thr
levels of middle class, lower class, and other. Ninety-fiv
per cent of them chose the two categories within middle
class called "upper middle" and "middle."[17] These are th
two major divisions perceived by respondents, and for som
purposes we shall subsume the few "upper class" designee
into the "upper middle class" group and the one "lower mi
dle class" individual into the "middle class" category.

Referring to Table 3, we see that income and class
identification are related.[18] Three-quarters of those calli
themselves "upper class," a little over 60 per cent of the
"upper middle class," and less than 20 per cent of the "m
dle class" report incomes of Rs. 800 and above. All with
incomes below Rs. 300 call themselves "middle class."
Yet it should be noted that almost one-fifth of those in the
highest income group also consider themselves "middle
class." Respondents tend to evaluate their class position
in economic terms but differ somewhat in their standards
judgment.

Both the living costs and the income of a family flu
ate over time. The number of children attending schools
colleges has direct impact on family finances. The father
most likely to be the main source of financial support dur

the period that most of his children are being educated,
meeting the costs of tuition and books as well as living expenses.   However, once older brothers have finished college
and obtained employment, family income may go up dramatically.   The vast majority of respondents come from homes
in which at least one sibling has completed his or her education.   But at the same time, most have at least one sibling still in the process of being educated.

As an extreme example, one Brahmin woman with
seven well-educated elder brothers explained her family's
changed financial status by saying, "All my brothers studied
by getting scholarships and freeships.   In fact we were poor
and it was very difficult when my father died.   But now all
of them have come up. " This respondent lists family income in the highest category, and class as "upper middle"--
in spite of the fact that the family, including some married
brothers, resides in small and modest quarters.

According to one study, type of dwelling unit is a
relatively poor indicator of economic status, inasmuch as
most of the Bangalore population live in brick, stone or ce-
ment houses. [19] Hut dwellers are relatively small in number compared to some other cities, and none of our respondents is included among this group.   On the other hand,
houses vary considerably both in interior furnishings and exteriors.   As suggested in the beginning of the chapter, more
modest dwellings are characterized by such features as:
small number and size of rooms, little privacy from neighbors, external overcrowding of units, absence of gardens or
compounds, absence of fences and gates, the presence of
roaming animals close to the house and in some cases the
keeping of chickens within the hallways.   The well-to-do
representatives of Bangalore society, whom foreigners tend
to meet socially, possess more spacious compounds than almost all we encountered in the course of interviewing.   We
saw the exteriors of homes of three of the four respondents
who call themselves "upper class"; only that of the young
woman now residing in the United States, described earlier,
resembles in affluence the most fashionable homes found in
Bangalore. [20]

Most of the homes encountered had some kind of front
room in which visitors could be greeted, but these varied
greatly in furnishings and decor.   A chair was almost always produced for the foreign visitor, but occasionally mats
served for our Indian assistants.   A range in living standards

is obviously characteristic of the broad stratum considered
to be part of the middle class.

Because traditional attitudes toward women tend to be
more restrictive among Moslems, it might be expected that
highly-educated Moslem women represent a more westernized
elite group.   Personal visits to Moslem homes suggest otherwise, as does consideration of income and class.   The majority of both Moslems and Christians place themselves in
the "middle class"; the median income of both groups is between Rs. 300 and 499 although both exhibit a wide range.
In general, then, some level of middle class status charac-
terizes the non-Hindus as well as the Hindus.

We have looked at a number of indices of class: income, fathers' and mothers' occupations, own identification
of class, and characteristics of dwelling place.   Each by itself is not a conclusive indicator; taken together these facts
provide overwhelming evidence that we are dealing with a
middle class sample.   To repeat our beginning premise, college and graduate education is no longer the privilege of a
small elite group but has now become available to the growing numbers of urban middle class women.

If it is true that many members of the middle classes
feel economically pressed, the likelihood that a woman's education will lead to gainful employment is increased.   Kapadia
claims that this is happening:

> Under the pressure of economic necessity, opposi-
> tion to the gainful occupation of women is steadily
> diminishing.   The Second World War, and particu-
> larly the period after its close, hit the middle
> class so hard economically that this change in at-
> titude is shown even by members of the older gener-
> tion. [21]

Respondents were quick to give very exact information
on the educational level of their parents, except in a few
cases where fathers apparently had little education.

Table 4 contrasts the education of fathers and mothers. [22]   Forty-seven per cent of the fathers, as contrasted
with seven per cent of the mothers, had obtained one or more
college degrees.   More than half of the college-educated fathers hold two or more degrees.   In contrast, looking at the
lower levels of educational attainment, we find that only 7

per cent of the fathers but over 60 per cent of the mothers have not completed secondary school (tenth standard).

TABLE 4:   FATHERS AND MOTHERS OF RESPONDENTS
                BY EDUCATIONAL LEVEL

Highest Level Finished

	Father		Mother	
	No.	%	No.	%
College	45	47	7	7
Secondary school[a]	44	46	28	29
Below secondary school	7	7	61	64
Total[b]	96	100	96	100

a.   Or specialized language or music education.
b.   One respondent did not provide this information.

The pattern of highly educated men being married to rather uneducated spouses is quite common in India.   However, of the seven college-educated mothers, six are married to men with degrees, suggesting that the reverse pattern is unlikely to obtain.   We will see that this generation's college educated women expect to marry at least equally well-educated husbands, and they consider that being a "graduate" aids in doing so, even though most of their mothers did not find education necessary.

When middle-class girls were married during childhood, their education tended to be discontinued.   In consequence, such females were not prepared for respectable work outside the home.   The 11 mothers who have worked constitute a more highly educated group, almost three-quarters of them having finished secondary school or above, as contrasted to one-third of all mothers who have done so.   In addition, two have a specialized language education qualifying them to teach.   Of the seven mothers holding a college or medical degree, five are working or have worked.   The relationship of higher education to employment is apparently not a new phenomenon; more Indian women obtaining college degrees and hence becoming employed, is.

Considering the small percentage of Indian college graduates, the fathers represent a highly educated group. The mothers are more highly educated than the vast majority of Indian women in Mysore State. More than one-third of them finished seventh standard approximately two decades ago, when female education was even less usual. [23]

However, the contrast between respondents and their mothers is sharp. One hundred per cent of the younger women and only 7 per cent of their mothers hold college degrees. The relationships between these highly educated daughters and their mothers might well be worthy of study. Furthermore, when and if they marry, these graduates will have to relate deferentially to mothers-in-law whose educational background will probably resemble their mothers'.

Although fathers' education is not significantly related to income, it does tend to be associated with class identification. If her father does not have a college degree, his daughter is much more likely to classify the family as "middle" rather than "upper middle" class.

More than half of the sample comes from families in which there are five or more children (see Table 5). While the median number of both brothers and sisters is two, there are slightly more sisters than brothers. [24] Eighty-two women have one or more brothers while 84 have one or more sisters; only three individuals have no siblings. The relationship between number of siblings and caste or religion is not statistically significant. However, the families with more siblings have proportionately higher incomes than those with fewer siblings. [25] This fact is open to varying interpretations. Perhaps only large families which are also relatively well off can afford to keep their daughters in college. Or perhaps families with more children also tend to have some who are working and contributing to the household.

Educational information about brothers and sisters was given readily, in much detail as to type of degree, subjects studied and degree of merit attained. Since all but the poorest families send their children to some type of private school rather than to a government school, large families mean a continuous financial outlay over many years. Tuition rates in private schools vary tremendously, from a high charged at the most exclusive English medium schools to the low at neighborhood schools. More than a quarter of the families have other children in attendance at both colleges

TABLE 5: INCOME, CASTE AND RELIGION BY NUMBER OF RESPONDENTS' SIBLINGS

Number of Siblings	Total	Income in Rupees Monthly				Caste and Religion			
	No. (%)	Below 299 No. (%)	300-499 No. (%)	500-799 No. (%)	800 up No. (%)	Brahmin No. (%)	Other Hindu No. (%)	Moslem No. (%)	Christian No. (%)
3 or fewer	43 (44)	6 (86)	13 (52)	15 (45)	9 (28)	22 (43)	9 (41)	4 (44)	8 (53)
4 or more	54 (56)	1 (14)	12 (48)	18 (55)	23 (72)	29 (57)	13 (59)	5 (56)	7 (47)
Total	97	7	25	33	32	51	22	9	15

and lower schools, another quarter or so have other children studying below college level only, and another quarter have no other children currently studying.

The quest for higher education appears to be a family decision rather than an individual matter. Forty-six respondents have at least one sister who holds a college degree; 45 respondents have at least one brother with a degree. About one-quarter of the sample have at least one brother and one sister who are college-educated.

Eighteen individuals are the first members of their families, including their parents, to obtain a degree. How do they compare with the rest of the sample? Perhaps the most striking difference is in father's occupations. Whereas 70 per cent of all fathers are classified in professional and managerial occupations (Table 2), only one-third of these fathers are so classified. Seven of the total of nine fathers designated as having working class occupations are found in this group. One-third of the Christian respondents are the first in their families to obtain degrees, while this is true of less than one-seventh of the Brahmans and one-ninth of the Moslems. While the modal income is the same, between 500 and 799 rupees monthly, 44 per cent of the "first to be educated" have incomes below 500 rupees monthly as contrasted to 33 per cent of the total. Seventy-eight per cent of this group call themselves "middle-class" (rather than upper middle class or above) as compared to two-thirds of the total. Of the nine mothers who are either working or have worked, four are represented among this group. Without going into great detail as to the significance of these facts, it is obvious that the women who are first in their families to acquire an education come from lower socio-economic backgrounds than average and are upwardly mobile.

Educational information about 19 husbands and one future husband turns up only one who lacks a college degree. Three have only a B.A., B.Sc. or other diploma, with the remaining 80 per cent having more education or studying for advanced degrees. Eleven, or more than half, are doctors, lawyers or engineers, while four fall into the "other professional" category. Four are in the clerical or white collar group, while one is a manager. Thus, 80 per cent are in the professional or managerial class.

Questions about the persistence or dissolution of joint family living have been a matter of debate and concern among

social scientists, who view the joint family as intimately related to other traditional patterns. [26] The data on composition of households presented here add to the factual evidence
available on this question. However, questions were not
asked about the pooling of income or other such indices of
joint family life. To the extent that the joint family concept
includes members not residing in the household, the joint
family will be underrepresented in these figures.

The classification of family types employed by Ross
in her first Bangalore study, with some minor adjustments,
will be used so that the two samples can be compared. [27]
As she points out, an individual may live in several types
of family units during the course of his or her lifetime. Our
data is limited, of course, to the period in their lives represented by the average age of respondents.

Ross' classification is as follows: Type A is the
large joint family, distinguished from Type B by its genera-
tional depth. It includes three or more generations living
together in the same household, cooking in the same kitchen,
owning property in common and pooling their incomes for
common spending [Ross, p. 34]. A case is included in the
Type A category if members of three or more generations
are living together patrilocally, and regardless of whether
or not there are additional relatives in the household.

As can be seen in Table 6, 16 per cent of our respondents, but none of the married ones, are living in Type
A families.

Type B is the small joint family, defined by Ross
[p. 35] as "composed of a household in which parents live
with their married sons and other unmarried children, or
two brothers live together with their wives and children. A
family fitting this description may have one or more additional relatives in the household, but lacks more than two generations in depth. Thirteen per cent of the sample live in this
type of household. A little more than one-quarter of the
married women are living with in-laws in Type B families,
but none of the seven mothers is doing so. Nine of the
single women are living in small joint families.

Type C consists of the nuclear family, composed usually of one or both parents and their children. Almost three-
fifths of the respondents live in such family units.

TABLE 6:   SINGLE AND MARRIED RESPONDENTS
BY HOUSEHOLD TYPE

Family Type	Single		Married		Total	
	No.	(%)	No.	(%)	No.	(%)
A (large joint family)	15	20	0	0	15	16
B (small joint family)	7	9	5	26	12	13
C (nuclear)	41	54	13	68	54	57
D (nuclear with dependents)	13	17	1	5	14	15
	76	100	19	99	95	100

Type D: "the nuclear family with dependents consists of parents, their children and one or more dependents. " A person is considered a dependent when he "has no authority or responsibility in family matters" [Ross, p. 36].   In setting up this category, Ross appears to have in mind such individuals as unmarried sisters or widows living in a brother's home; a brother who is earning and contributing is likely to be considered a "true" household member.   Thus, the presence of the earning brother would tend to make this a small joint family, Type B.

Here we shall differ slightly from the above usage by including as a Type D nuclear family any one which has one or more odd relatives other than those in the nuclear unit living in the home.   The distinction between Type B and Type D is sometimes difficult to make, and when in doubt we classify the family as Type D.   Thus, although a young woman may be earning and contributing to the household, she is still thought of as under the protection of her brother and dependent on him socially.   Four single women, living in homes other than those of their own parents, are classified in Type D.   Three cases occur in which brothers-in-law reside with their wives, sisters of our respondents, and in-laws.   These men are appendages to nuclear families in which they have no well-defined role, and are therefore classified as dependents.   In seven additional families other relatives are living as dependents, so that this type of unit totals 15 per cent of the households.

Considering that Ross' sample of Bangalore families was obtained in a different manner from the present one, and more than ten years earlier, the obvious similarities in data are noteworthy.   Looking at Table 7, we see that almost half

of her respondents and 57 per cent of ours report living in
nuclear family units.   Both samples show 16 per cent or
less living in the large joint family, Type A.   Type B is
more prominent in the Ross sample, and is probably only
partly accounted for by our difference in classification.

TABLE 7:   COMPARISON OF HOUSEHOLD TYPES
OF TWO BANGALORE SAMPLES

Family Type	Goldstein Sample		Ross Sample[a]	
	No.	%	No.	%
A (large joint family)	15	16	19	13
B (small joint family)	12	13	44	28
C (nuclear)	54	57	77	49
D (nuclear with dependents)	14	15	17	11
Totals[b]	95	101	157	101

a.   Totals abstracted from Aileen B. Ross, The Hindu
     Family in Its Urban Setting, Table XIII, p. 303.
b.   Of the two respondents not included, one is a nun living
     in a religious order; the other gave no information.

Perhaps most significant is the prevalence of the nuclear household in both studies.   The education of members of
the samples and their male relatives probably is at least partially responsible.   Higher education makes spatial mobility
more likely, and many husbands of respondents work in lo-
calities other than where their parents reside.   They may
well be contributing to their parents' household financially
and also entering into decision-making about important matters such as the marriage of sisters.   In this sense, they
are still part of the joint family, even though they are not
involved in day-to-day decisions.

Life expectancy also enters into the picture.   By the
time an Indian reaches adulthood, one or both parents may
be deceased.   The death of parents will tend to push unmarried women into the household of their brothers, thus increasing the number of Type B households.   At the same
time, the pressure on married brothers and their families
to maintain a joint residence does not appear to be as strong
as that to remain with parents.

Christians differ from other groups in the sample in that all but one of the families live in nuclear units, and that one is a "nuclear family with dependents." While Moslems and Christians resemble each other in having slightly lower incomes on the average than the Hindus, Moslems also have a joint family system, comparable to that of the Hindus. Income is slightly related to household type, but the relationship is not statistically significant. The small joint families are more highly represented among those with higher incomes, while the nuclear families have a higher proportion of lower income families. The small joint family often includes adult brothers and hence more contributors to family income. Further study is needed to explore these relationships.

In summary, the average woman who is the subject of this book is single, 22 years old, comes from a highly educated middle class group, has four brothers and sisters, and has a family income of between 500 and 799 rupees monthly; in addition, she is more than 50 per cent likely to reside in a nuclear family unit, 44 per cent likely to be employed, and almost 33 per cent likely to be studying for an advanced degree.

Notes

1. Matriculate is one who has finished secondary school, tenth standard (grade).

2. The Cantonment refers to the former Civil and Military Station, that part of Bangalore which was under British administration, in contrast to the part which belonged to the princely state. In 1947 the two parts were merged to form the Bangalore Corporation.

3. Seventh standard (grade).

4. Intermediate and Senior Cambridge both consist or consisted of an 11th year following secondary school, and before college.

5. These figures are assumed to represent, roughly, the proportions of females from these religious groups who were graduated from Bangalore University in 1965. A fairly recent estimate of the religious

population of Bangalore city is as follows: Hindu,
75. 5 per cent; Moslem, 15. 0 per cent; and Christian,
9. 6 per cent [The Mysore Population Study (New
York: United Nations, 1961), table 7. 1, p.   56].
Because of the small number of Moslem and Christian
respondents, religion will not be used as a major
variable.

6.   Two women are unpaid religious workers: one, a
     Catholic nun, and the other, the daughter of a re-
     tired Protestant minister.

7.   André Béteille classifies these groups as Brahmins,
     non-Brahmins and a third group known by the various
     names of Adi-Dravida, Untouchables, or Harijans.
     Caste, Class and Power (Berkeley: University of
     California Press, 1965), p. 15.   Béteille's "non-
     Brahmin" group is sometimes classified as Shudras.
     For example, A. L. Basham states, "While brah-
     mins and sudras are to be found in nearly all Hindu
     communities, there are some parts of India, espe-
     cially in the south of the sub-continent, where
     ksatriyas and vaisyas are hardly to be found at
     all. "   "Indian Society and the Legacy of the Past, "
     Australian Journal of Politics and History 12 (1966):
     134.   Others object to the term Shudra, as pejora-
     tive and inaccurate.

8.   G. S. Ghurye, Caste and Race in India (Bombay: Popu-
     lar Prakishan, 5th ed. , 1969), ch. 8. ; David G.
     Mandelbaum, Society in India, vol. 1, Continuity and
     Change (Berkeley: University of California Press,
     1970), ch. 2.

9.   These are, of course, the Brahmins, the Kshatriyas,
     the Vaisyas, and the Sudras.   (Slightly different
     spellings of some of these terms appear in various
     reputable sources.)

10. See A. P. Barnabas and Subhash C. Mehta, Caste in
     Changing India (New Delhi: Indian Institute of Public
     Administration, 1965), pp. 72-74.   In academic ad-
     missions, reservation of seats for "backward classes"
     usually operates within that group of candidates which
     has attained the minimum prescribed qualifications
     but does not score high enough to be selected on
     merit [ibid, p. 56].   P. M. Menon writes, "It has

been estimated ... that of 140, 000 graduates turned out each year only 2 per cent belong to scheduled castes and scheduled tribes. " "Towards Equality of Opportunity in India, " International Labour Review 94, no. 4 (October 1966): 368.

11. George Rosen, Democracy and Economic Change in India (Berkeley: University of California Press, 1966), p. 38.

12. B. B. Misra, The Indian Middle Classes: Their Growth in Modern Times (London: Oxford Universit) Press, 1961), p. 13.

13. Rosen, op. cit., pp. 38-39.

14. In a recent study, P. N. Pimpley and K. Anand found that educated men seemed to prefer as wives women engaged mainly in three occupations, i. e. , teachers, lecturers and doctors. They conclude "This may be because only these three occupations are considered to be reputable occupations for women. " "Role of Occupation in Marital Alliances, " Indian Journal of Social Work 25, no. 4 (January, 1965): 388.

15. Rosen, op. cit. , p. 189.

16. Several respondents or their fathers discussed the problems of early retirement ages for government employees. Some fathers who had held responsible positions were unwilling to seek other work not deemed "suitable. "

17. The respondent who called herself lower middle class did so in a very deliberate way. The interviewer writes, "At first she said that she belongs to the middle class, but later said that taking into consideration the income and living conditions she would consider her family to belong to the lower middle class. " Apparently respondents did not like to desig nate themselves as "lower" middle class.

18. If we dichotomize both income and class identification into two categories, the relationship between them is significant at the . 01 level, the sum of Chi-square = 16. 919, d. f. = 1. (Income is divided into above and below Rs. 500 monthly; the small categories of

upper class and lower middle class, respectively are combined with the two middle categories, upper middle and middle class.)

19.   The Mysore Population Study, op. cit., p. 61.

20.   Had we been concerned more specifically with determining class, other indices could have been developed; for example, the possession of a telephone, car or motor-scooter. Interior living space is probably a poor index because the presence of married brothers with wives and children tends to overcrowd homes. Emphasis on educating one's children would seem to be another class indicator, but this is complicated by the relationship of caste and religion to educational values.

21.   K. M. Kapadia, Marriage and Family in India, 3rd, ed. rev. (Bombay: Oxford University Press, 1966), p. 265. Rosen details the changing economic position of the middle classes in the decade of the 1950's. He estimates that the lower middle class, defined as white-collar employees with incomes below 300 rupees per month, has doubled in numbers between 1951 and 1961 (op. cit., p. 189-190). Regarding their rising expectations, he states, "... it is possible that there is now a wider gap between the expectations of this larger group and their accomplishments than there was previously, since many have not received the great opportunities they thought their education opened to them; and this is a source of potential political unrest. This gap would, naturally, be greatest among the educated unemployed" [p. 190].

22.   A variety of nomenclatures is used in Indian states to denote the various stages of education. To simplify, such terms as "matriculate" or "intermediate" have been translated into the number of standards (grades) completed, according to the usage of these terms in Bangalore and taking into account modifications in terminology over the years.

23.   Figures on current enrollment of girls, as percentage of the corresponding age group, show that 4.8 per cent of girls in Mysore State are enrolled in grades 9 to 11, while 12.5 per cent are enrolled in grades

6 to 8. Education and National Development (New
Delhi: Government of India Press, 1966), p. 126,
table 6. 6.

24. Other studies might investigate the relationship between
high educational level and the presence of sisters.
Are different roles assigned to various sisters?
One respondent attributed her parents' refusal to
allow her to study medicine to the fact that she was
the only daughter. A contrasting hypothesis, which
our evidence points to, is that the presence of educated older siblings of either sex facilitates the education of younger ones.

25. Dichotomizing income levels into those above and below
Rs. 500 per month, and number of siblings into
above and below 4, Chi-square = 4. 73, d. f. = 1
which is significant at the . 05 level.

26. See for example, "Symposium on Joint Family, " Sociological Bulletin 4, no. 2 (September 1955).

27. Aileen D. Ross, The Hindu Family in Its Urban Setting
(Toronto: University of Toronto Press, 1961).

Chapter III

STUDENTS IN SARIS:
THE MEANING OF EDUCATION

The advance made in elevating the position of Indian women in this century has been remarkable or unimpressive, depending on one's standard. Compared to a mythical society in which women have perfect equality with men, their progress has been infinitesimal. Compared to modern American counterparts, there is room for change. But compared to their own condition, a comparatively few years ago, their progress has been rapid.

Beatrice Pitney Lamb still considers the status of Indian women to be an unhappy one. She summarizes it this way:

> Although her legal position has been greatly improved, the Hindu woman, except in Westernized circles, is still bound by ancient traditions of behavior that emphasize her submission, obedience, devotion, and absolute dedication to her husband and his every wish. Her husband is almost a god, and the home is her life and her career....
> Among the tiny emancipated Westernized minority, there are many outstanding and forceful women prominent in public life....
> But such women are the exceptions. The vast majority are far less educated than the Indian men. In 1961, the rate of literacy among women was less than half that among men. Because women still generally follow tradition, successive generations of Indian children--even those of Westernized fathers--learn the old values and modes of thought from the womenfolk who bring them up. This is another reason for the tenacious hold of many old customs and for the continued coexistence of the new and old. [1]

Writing at the same time, the Indian sociologist, K.
M. Kapadia paints a more optimistic picture:

> The rapid strides in higher education during the
> last twenty-five years have exercised their impact
> in two ways, first by creating conditions for a
> woman to be self-reliant and secondly by creating
> stronger emotional bonds between her and her hus-
> band. An educated young man is no longer satis-
> fied with the prospect of a wife who can only be
> the acquiescent slave of his desires and the be-
> getter of his children, but looks for intellectual
> cooperation and participation in the pleasures and
> joys of life. The educated wife is expected to be
> a companion who will share his interests, go with
> him to clubs and films, sports and parties, and
> thus be united emotionally with him. This new
> concept of wifehood, which is associated with ur-
> ban living, has assigned to the wife a new status
> in the family, even if it be joint. [2]

Lamb and Kapadia are both right, from their own
perspectives. The negative, culturally biased Lamb view
which equates Westernization with progress is borne out by
statistics on illiteracy and level of education of women in
absolute terms. However, as has been demonstrated ob-
jectively, a narrowing of the differences in educational level
between men and women has taken place in the last 25 years.
And we have already indicated the vast difference in educational attainments of respondents and their mothers.

In contrast, Degler and others show that the educational position of women in the United States has been re-
gressing. Women constituted almost 40 per cent of students
in American institutions of higher learning in 1937 but only
35 per cent in 1952-53. The present ratio of women to men
students in India is 1:4, a figure closely resembling that in
the Sweden of 1952-53. [3]

Both Lamb and Kapadia link women's education with
their status in the family and in society at large. Of course
they are correct in doing so. Since a daughter's marriage
is of prime concern to the family, all of her behavior is
judged in terms of its effects on her chances (and those of
her sisters) for making a "suitable" marriage. Other goals
such as education take second place, even though a few exceptions to this traditional emphasis can be seen.

How is it, then, that the young women interviewed claim higher education to be their major aspiration, at least for the immediate future? When asked what they would like to do in the next two years if they had absolutely free choice, respondents most frequently selected educational aims. In actuality, 30 per cent of the sample are engaged in study for higher degrees, with an additional 28 per cent hoping or planning to continue their education. Of the remainder, almost one-third already hold higher degrees. In all, less than three-tenths of the sample definitely expect to finish their education with a bachelor's degree. [4] Table 8 shows separately the educational aspirations and activities of the less highly educated and more educated respondents.

The strong and open commitment to education voiced by these young women could not have occurred without the support of family and community members. Asked, "Which family members have most strongly influenced decisions about your education?" they designate their fathers alone or in combination with other family members almost two-thirds of the time. Mothers are named slightly less than two-fifths of the time, and brothers are third in influence. In almost half of the cases, more than one family member had strongly influenced decisions, showing that the daughter's education is often a matter for family discussion. Seven per cent of respondents claim that continuing their education was their own choice, without specific influence from others.

This strong family encouragement suggests that higher education may now be viewed as a help rather than a hindrance in marriage, at least by these families. A Bangalore "graduate, " visiting her kinship group in a village, is still likely to face the conservative attitudes and suspicion that attach to an educated woman. But in the main she believes that college education is more likely to help her in obtaining a mate than not, or at least that it will not affect her marriage chances negatively. Chapter IV discusses her reasoning in more detail, but Table 9 shows the responses, by educational level, to the question, "Do you think that education helps or hinders in finding a suitable partner?" The less educated respondents have a slightly more favorable opinion about the role of education in marital choice. [5]

The early advocates of "female education" suffered much criticism; today its opponents are considered old-fashioned and are fewer in number. To understand why, the new conditions facilitating education and the modifications

TABLE 8: EDUCATIONAL LEVEL OF RESPONDENTS BY CURRENT ACTIVITIES AND PLANS

Educational Activities	Present Educational Level					
	Total		Less Educated[a]		Highly Educated[b]	
	No.	%	No.	%	No.	%
Now studying for advanced degree	29	30	27	40	2	7
Planning to do further studies	27	28	13	19	14	50
Not planning further studies	40	42	28	41	12	43
Total	96	100	68	100	28	100

a. "Less educated," in terms of present educational level, includes those holding only a B.A. or B.Sc.

b. "Highly educated" includes those who hold master's, double-bachelor's, medical, and law degrees.

of certain traditional sentiments surrounding it must be examined. This is not to say there is unanimity about how much education is good for a woman.

TABLE 9: WOMEN BY PRESENT EDUCATIONAL LEVEL AS THEY VIEW ROLE OF EDUCATION IN FINDING A MATE

Role of Education	Total No.	(%)	Less Educated No.	(%)	Highly Educated No.	(%)
Helps	60	(63)	47	(68)	13	(50)
Hinders	8	(8)	3	(4)	5	(19)
Neither; or, sometimes helps, sometimes hinders	27	(28)	19	(28)	8	(31)
Total	95	(99)	69	(100)	26	(100)

Reforms centering around the improvement of women's position and their consequences have played an important role. Among the related factors to be examined are (1) the abolition of child marriage and its consequences for education; (2) the compulsory nature of marriage for women; (3) the notion of women's perpetual tutelage and the need for male protection; (4) the need to keep women busy, as related to beliefs about their sexuality; (5) the importance of gossip and reputation; (6) the notion of individual nature; (7) the lack of alternatives to college attendance; and (8) the intrinsic value of education for the young woman. The greatest impediment to the education of girls was child-marriage, as Thomas indicates in this passage:

> As long as child-marriage was the general rule, it was difficult to make any appreciable progress towards the spread of female education, as among the better classes of Hindus, girls were married before they were old enough to learn the three Rs, and the lower classes were not interested in female education. But in 1929, the Prohibition of Child-Marriage Act... raised the minimum age for marriage of girls to fourteen. Once the old convention, that a girl had to be married before menstruation, was overcome, marriage did not always take place at the age of fourteen;

in fact girls grew into young ladies of seventeen
or eighteen before marriage proposals started
coming in, and all that the parents could do, in
the meantime, was to let their daughters continue
their studies till marriage. And it even became
fashionable for parents, whose daughters were remaining for want of desirable proposals coming in
or for want of cash to provide dowry, to give out
the plausible explanation that the girls were so
passionately fond of their studies that it was im-
possible to put ideas of marriage into their heads.

Thus, as Thomas points out, the abolition of child
marriage was a crucial factor in opening up the alternative
of education to the female child. Without the deadline of
puberty, fathers could pursue a more leisurely course in
obtaining bridegrooms for their daughters. The high cost
of marriages and dowry, coupled with other economic pressures, tended to push the marriage age up, and education
could become the justification.

Tradition had held that the only sure way of protecting a girl's chastity was to marry her off before puberty.
Postponing marriage and providing her with more education
might make a girl intractable, and less able to adjust to her
husband and in-laws. However, the tradition of child marriage and one of its unfortunate consequences, child-widow-
hood, was to come under attack by certain reformers. Altekar maintains that "secular causes" or conditions also
favored raising the age at marriage and that some members
of the "advanced middle classes" had already adopted this
practice before the 1929 passage of the Sarda Act. [7]

Whatever the secular causes, which Altekar does not
describe, a long list of illustrious reformers provided ideological support for the Act. Individuals and groups continued
their vigorous condemnation of child marriage after the law's
passage, cognizant that the law alone did not insure change.
Reformers not only pointed out the cruelties involved in
child marriage, such as high maternity and infant mortality
rates and the curse of early widowhood, [8] but they also
stressed its impact on female education. Recalling more
glorious days in Indian history, feminist leaders such as
Annie Besant deplored the state of ignorance into which Indian women had fallen. [9] The uneducated (often illiterate) nar-
row and provincial mother, through her strong family influence, was said to hamper desired social changes. Mahatma

Gandhi castigated those men who would marry child-brides
as motivated by lust, and counselled young men to disobey
parents who would force them into such marriages. [10]

Gandhi tied the amelioration of women's condition to
the national welfare.   Raising the age at marriage and im-
proving the education of women became bound in with other
major goals, such as the abolition of sati, [11] the mitigation
of caste inequality, and the gaining of national independence.

There is no doubt that reform in marriage age has
come about, especially in cities.   In Bangalore, the caste
most orthodox in these matters, middle class Brahmins, no
longer feel obliged to marry their daughters before puberty.
Less than one-fifth of the respondents, whose median age is
22, are married.   Young women's views about the desirability of later marriage will be discussed in Chapter IV.   While
the rise in age at marriage is less dramatic in rural areas,
it has occurred.   According to the 1961 census, 77.7 per
cent of rural girls age 10 to 14 had never been married.
The corresponding figure for urban girls was 93.1.   Table
10 shows the marital status of rural and urban females for
three age categories.   Only three per cent of urban women
have never been married by age 34, but interestingly enough,
about one-quarter of them are married between the ages of
25 and 34.

TABLE 10*: MARITAL STATUS (1961) OF INDIAN FEMALES
           BY AGE GROUP--PERCENTAGES

Age group	Rural/ Urban	Never Married	Married	Widowed	Divorced
10-14	R	77.7	22.0	.2	.1
	U	93.1	6.8	.1	
15-24	R	14.2	84.0	1.0	.8
	U	29.4	69.4	.7	.5
25-34	R	1.2	93.2	4.6	1.0
	U	3.0	92.2	3.9	.9

*From The Gazetteer of India, vol. 1, Country and People
(Govt. of India Publications Division, 1965); adapted from
Table 8, p. 529.

It is obvious that, after graduating from high school at about 15 or 16 years of age, young women have a gap of time to "fill" before marriage.

Because the relationship between Indian husband and wife has traditionally been sex-centered, the physically mature young woman is expected to keep herself from thinking about marriage. [12] The motto, "An idle mind is the Devil's companion," was quoted by both Christian and non-Christian respondents, as they discussed the need to keep busy. Keeping fully occupied will allow the young woman little time for thoughts of marriage.

Several authors have commented on the problem of filling in time between high school graduation and marriage. Ross sees this as a factor motivating parents to send their daughters to college, stating:

> Perhaps one of the main reasons for this new trend is that, with the change from child to adult marriage, the leisure time of girls must now be filled in up to nineteen or even twenty-five years. And college is one way of 'keeping them busy' until marriage. [13]

Mehta makes the same observation about the educated women she studied, indicating that they went to college as an "accident" rather than as part of a plan:

> They continued their education because there was really no alternative except marriage. Since marriage at the age of fifteen or sixteen was not an acceptable alternative to their fathers, the logical thing was to send them to college. Also, the small family unit of their parents did not have the same means to keep the adolescent occupied as in a large family. [14]

In contrast, Kapadia stresses the need for education as a reason for now setting the marriage age at 20 or above as follows:

> Education has become necessary for a female not only for marriage but for her economic independence. A college education is desired if the female is to be a worthy partner in marriage. Girls do not generally matriculate before the age of 16. Grant

ing at least four years for a college education, a
girl would not be ready for marriage before 20,
and hence this is a desirable age for marriage. [15]

Fathers and male relatives have a religious duty to
protect the women of the family, Altekar explains:

As a woman herself has observed in the Mahab-
harata, to be without a proper protector is a great
calamity of the fair sex in this world, which is
full of wickedness. Manu therefore ordains that
the father ought to protect a woman while she is
a maiden, the husband when she is married, and
the sons when the husband is no more; a woman
ought not to remain independent. In the immediately next verse Manu points out that the father
would be to blame if he does not marry his daughter in the proper time, the husband, if he does
not look after his wife properly, and the son, if
he does not protect his mother during her old
age. [16]

How is it then, that young women are allowed to attend college, to go out into the world without a male protector? This norm about chaperonage and male protection is
in a transitional stage in Bangalore, with certain compro-
mises being allowed in order that education be obtained.
The same individual who travels to college alone, or alone
for part of the way, may be restricted from doing so to
recreational activities. A college student or graduate may
be allowed to attend the cinema only if accompanied by a
male relative. This necessity for companionship is rarely
questioned; rather it seems that many women truly fear
traveling alone. There is little disagreement among observers that a woman who travels alone is sometimes subject to
teasing, harassment, or worse. The most frequent substitute for male chaperonage, and one that young women seem
to prefer as less restrictive, is the company of classmates
or friends.

Only a few respondents admit that their parents object
to co-education at the graduate school level. Remarks such
as, "They trust me" or "They know I know right from
wrong," suggest that the college educated woman is beginning to be accorded a certain amount of independence from
male protection.

Just as the advantages of college education appear to outweigh traditional concerns about chaperonage, so there are indications that good jobs can sometimes entice women to travel daily by public transportation. On the other hand, distance from home can be determinative of whether a daughter will be permitted to take a particular job or attend a particular college, depending on the "conservatism" of her family.

Social pressure, expressed through gossip, and community estimate of reputation, continues to exert much influence. Considering the anonymity usually associated with city life, how is it that "what people say" is still vitally significant to the urban families represented in this sample?

The circle of individuals who are involved in and concerned about the activities of a particular family may be relatively small. Members of the endogamous community know and gossip about one another. It is this community to which respondents refer when talking about the effects of education or employment on marital chances. Girl-watching is practiced not only by boys but by elders and neighbors of all kinds. Since the good reputation of the woman is essential in making marriage arrangements, fear of gossip is strong. In the process of locating mates for their children, parents or third parties make many inquiries about potential candidates. Thus the importance of hearsay is great, especially since some families may falsify the information advanced about their marriageable children.

Not only do the comments of neighbors and friends serve as character references, but they also carry weight in decision-making. Neighbors may enter into the process of convincing the family of a contemplated course of action, including that of sending a daughter to college. To the extent that the social climate favors higher education for women, the family will be encouraged to educate its girls. A "love marriage" known to be under discussion for over a year was finally permitted by the widowed mother of the man involved, after age peers had convinced her it was the wise thing to do. This case demonstrates that friends and neighbors can sometimes provide support for a potentially unpopular decision. The mother who agreed to an intercaste "love marriage" had already received assurances that she would be supported rather than criticized.

The maintenance of position is, of course, involved

in concern about reputation. The hierarchical nature of Indian society affects non-Hindus as well as Hindus. Each marriage must be arranged with extreme care as to its suitability. Individuals are matched in terms of caste, education, and sometimes class. The prospective bride's looks and her accomplishments in homemaking, music and other arts are taken into account while the man's education and occupation are most important. An unequal marriage is much talked about and a reflection on the family status.

As pointed out in the passage by Thomas referred to previously, a girl's strong interest in education may be functional for both herself and her parents. Any delay in arranging her marriage can be ascribed to the daughter's passionate interest in learning. If the father is having difficulty in arranging a match, his daughter may conveniently request a delay in order to continue her studies. On the other hand, should a good match be found there is every likelihood that it will be made immediately. At least seven of the 18 married respondents had finished their degrees after marriage. If chances for marriage become increasingly slim, the daughter may provide a face-saving device for her father by publicly indicating her deep devotion to a career or her lack of "a feeling for marriage."

A society which has strong prescriptions regarding family roles must also provide some safety valves. Some allowance for deviation from prescribed roles is afforded by the notion of individual nature, a term which includes more than temperament or personality alone and which recognizes a unique aspect to each individual.

The existence of differences in individual nature are recounted in stories of famous Indian women. These heroines are described as colorful and sometimes willful people, who are able to manifest their own distinctiveness while outwardly adjusting to the wishes of others. That a dutiful wife can also be a strong personality is well exemplified in her husband's account of the modern Indian heroine, Saroj Nalini. [17] (It also suggests that within women's formally prescribed roles there are opportunities for more or less effective role-playing.) Respondents include the factor of individual nature as one which must be taken into account in family decisions about a daughter. The concept is employed when referring to such matters as the type of job or husband suitable for a particular woman, her willfulness or meekness, and her suitability for marriage. The term is used frequently

in describing a wife's duty to adjust to her husband's nature.
A woman who is intent on further education may be able to
convince her parents to permit it; and if other community
members disapprove, the latter can point to the girl's nature
and persistence.   A woman who is considered "strong-willed"
will often be able to exert more influence on her own fate
than can a more timid sister.

Because education is a respected and respectable value, young women sometimes show some boldness in asking
parental permission to continue.   But, as in the following
two cases, different degrees of persistence may bring about
different results.   Two young Brahmins, one successful and
the other unsuccessful in their quest for graduate education,
describe their attempts in this way:

> Mother was very much against my studying in a co-
> educational college.   That's why she didn't want me
> to study for my M. A.   It took me a year to con-
> vince her.   My family is quite old-fashioned.   My
> mother felt that if I went to a co-educational col-
> lege there would be functions which I might have
> to attend, and the problem of transport, and a lot
> of undesirable things.   I might be dropped home
> by boys, or have boys to the house.   She's very
> much against mixing with boys.   But fortunately,
> she got me my own conveyance [a motor-scooter]
> so now I can be completely independent.

In contrast, the unsuccessful woman states:

> I wanted to continue but somehow my parents
> weren't in favor of it.   They preferred that I get
> married instead.   I was very keen on doing an
> M. B. B. S. (medical degree).   I was first class
> when I matriculated and was accepted for M. B. B. S.
> but they wouldn't allow....   At first, every time I
> thought of the M. B. B. S. I felt so bad, but now I
> am beginning to adjust.   I am quite meek and I
> will do what my parents say....   Many girls will
> do what they want, but I am not that way.

Apart from early marriage, there are few alternatives
to "putting" a daughter in college.   Appropriate employment
opportunities for less-educated girls are extremely limited,
and young high school graduates would be considered too
vulnerable to be permitted to work away from home.   House-

hold tasks, music lessons and needlework cannot fill all of
the daughter's time. As the acquisition of the degree gains
more prestige in the marriage market, college becomes a
desirable and visible way of occupying time. The cost of a
college education is not exhorbitant and the middle class
family, accustomed to paying tuition for secondary education,
comes to think of it as an expected burden. The student
can live at home, and as long as she returns at the proper
hour, she may be presumed to have spent the day safely at
college. Later the parents are faced with the question of
whether or not their daughter should be allowed to continue
for post-graduate work or to take a position. They know
that a post-graduate is more likely to be educated out of the
marriage market than a single graduate; yet, if a husband
has not yet been found, the easiest course once again is
more education. The young woman is usually willing to
accept this solution.

Since the female is not actively involved in seeking
her mate, her own attitudes toward education need not be
tied to considerations about marriage. She is expected to
maintain disinterest in marriage until it is upon her. Asked
whether they would advise the hypothetical sister of a friend
to enter college, 85 per cent of the respondents give uncon-
ditionally positive responses. The following is a spontane-
ous description of what college life means to one Indian girl
(mentioned just previously as unsuccessful in her desire to
pursue an M. B. B. S. degree):

> College is the best part of our lives. We are so
> free to move with people. We get ideas, our
> minds are broadened. There is much to adjust
> to at college and we learn to adjust. It is good
> for us. We can see our friends every day. Now
> my friends are working or taking post-graduate
> work, and we don't see each other very much.
> They live far from me. But in college it's so
> exciting. It's the best time of our lives, I feel.
> Now this is different, this studying at home. I
> told you I don't go to the cinema very much. Many
> girls go. But I am allowed only to go with a
> member of the family.... My father never goes.
> My mother doesn't get out much. If some of the
> family is visiting I may go. Otherwise, my father
> doesn't allow me to go with other girls. He is
> quite orthodox.

Clearly, the woman who has attended college finds
"sitting at home" a highly uninteresting prospect. This need
not imply that she is career-oriented or even interested in
the subjects she is studying. As is true in other countries,
young women have mixed motivations for attending college.
The following frank confession was made by a young lady
who is now a college lecturer:

> I only became interested in zoology after taking
> my M. Sc. My father wanted me to get married
> right after my B. Sc. , but I didn't want, so I took
> up the M. Sc. But I was not interested in the sub-
> ject. I only went to college to have good times,
> and many of us did. I had no thought of continuing
> so I thought, if I get a third class, it's good
> enough. I thought that I would never use my edu-
> cation. I was lucky enough to get a second class,
> so I got a place and could go on.

Attendance at college, then, has certain intrinsic rewards in the form of greater freedom, the opportunity to
see friends each day, and to have "good times." The result
of this inquiry do not tally with that of Ross, who claimed
that Bangalore women attend college for two main reasons:
to increase their marriage chances, and to relieve boredom.[1]
It is agreed that the young woman tends to find staying at
home "boring" after she has experienced college. But these
data suggest that further education may be preferred to some
proposed match. The motivations of parents and their daughters must be differentiated; the parents may consider education an appropriate time-filler until a suitable mate is found,
but the young woman may often hope for a few more years
of freedom before settling down to the wifely role.

Ross found that young women were less interested in
college and studied less than did their male counterparts. [19]
While this may be partly attributable to the fact that the necessity to secure jobs is more crucial for males, other
reasons may also be involved. For example, women may
not have to study as diligently as the particular male students with whom they are in competition. The most able
and affluent young men will most likely specialize in medicine and engineering, regardless of their interests, and will
probably not attend liberal arts colleges. These colleges
are considered highly appropriate for women, and may well
attract some with more ability than their male fellow student
Furthermore, the quality of teaching at Indian colleges some

times leaves much to be desired.   The young instructor previously quoted pointed out that her interest in her subject
had developed in spite of the poor way in which classes had
been taught.

Some of those who would allow women an education
suggest that it be a preparation for homemaking.   The major fields of study chosen by members of our sample will be
viewed to see if this is their guiding philosophy.   There are,
of course, a number of factors limiting choice of major.
Certain "combinations" such as English and social science,
or botany and zoology are offered together as majors.   Too,
the student has already made a choice between arts and sciences during her secondary school career and is likely to
continue in the same general area.   Her choice of college
major and of graduate work is likely to be limited to what
is offered at a local college, if this is the one her parents
have chosen.   As an example, one respondent who professed
interest in psychology was not allowed to attend an out-of-
town college where it was offered, and settled for sociology
for her master's degree--a not unusual compromise even in
the United States!

It is interesting that almost half of the respondents
report sciences or mathematics as the major subjects stud-
ed for their first degree, while a little over 40 per cent
majored in English or social sciences.   Only 10 per cent
majored in home science (home economics), the field which
would best prepare them for homemaking, and 2 per cent
took a degree in medicine.

Of those taking second degrees, the largest number
(34 per cent) have selected mathematics and science.   The
next field in popularity, accounting for a little more than a
quarter of the group, is education, with English and social
sciences almost as popular.   To qualify for better teaching
posts, a bachelor of education degree is frequently taken
after the bachelor of arts or bachelor of science degrees.
As teaching is considered the most appropriate work for
young women, this interest in obtaining an education degree
is not surprising.   However, those who are going on for
master's degrees in science, social science or English will
eventually quality for posts as college lecturers.   Although
it is unusual, a third class master's degree may even qualify
one for such a job.   A Christian acquaintance we knew, who
held a third class degree, was hired as a lecturer by a
Christian college.   Major fields other than those mentioned

above (home science and law, e.g.) account for 11 per cent of the sample members acquiring advanced degrees.

Advanced study does not appear to be associated with income. Forty per cent or more of the young women in each income category have already obtained higher degrees or are now studying for them. Five of the seven women with incomes below 300 rupees per month are in this more highly educated group, the largest percentage for any of the income categories. For such families, the woman's education is likely to be a way of bettering its economic circumstances. But how does one account for the fact mentioned earlier, that less than 30 per cent of the sample expect or want their education to end with the bachelor's degree? Our interpretation is that college-going produces its own impetus for continuing--as the most natural thing--once the initial degree has been attained, and if a husband has not been found.

Increased education may have diminishing returns as far as the marriageability of an Indian woman is concerned. Those who have done research on the subject hold different viewpoints about the degree of education considered desirable but the disagreement may be related to when the study was done. The question is, how educated a wife does an educated man want? In a study done more than 15 years ago, Margaret Cormack draws the line at matriculation:

> The tradition is growing that 'a girl must go to school if she wants a chance for a good marriage. Hence even modern education remains, for the Hindu girl, a road to marriage. All informants agreed that a girl betters her marriage chances by going up to Matriculation [roughly the equivalent of high school] but that increasingly the penalty of higher education is the decrease of marriage chances. [20]

Kapadia's viewpoint, that college education is valuable in the marriage market as well as essential for women's independence, has already been cited. In her most recent study, Ross notes the growing acceptance of education but maintains that there is a residue of fear and resistance to it:

> It is... probable that on the whole there is still much more resistance to higher education for

women (in India than elsewhere). Many Indians
still see it as useless luxury, as it is not expected
to be an asset to a married woman, and marriage is still their chief goal. ... Western parents are... aware that eligible husbands may be
found through co-education, whereas the Indian
parent is afraid that co-education may possibly
end in a dreaded 'love' marriage, and in any
case, as they are responsible for finding the
girl a husband, they feel they do not get any
assistance in this matter from their college
participation. [21]

Certainly these sentiments are still held by many
people. The more conservative fear that too much education
will "spoil" a girl. Nonetheless, study towards a bachelor's
degree is becoming increasingly acceptable and functional for
urban middle class women. Much more concern is expressed by parents regarding the advisability of post-graduate
study for females. A graduate wife may be sought by many
highly educated men, but a post-graduate is not likely to
have enhanced her marketability. In addition, the highly
educated woman requires a highly educated bridegroom and
dowry requirements for such men are often exhorbitant.

A Brahmin lecturer presents some of the dilemmas
well, in the following passage:

If it is arranged marriage, which is very common
in Bangalore, education helps in finding a suitable
partner. Many families want a girl with some
education. They will want a girl with a bachelor's
degree. But then they feel if a girl is highly educated, past B. A. , she won't know anything else,
about the home. They feel she will be too proud.
And if a girl is highly educated, she will have
ideas of her own, and it becomes very difficult.
She will naturally want a boy superior to her and
unless the family is very well off, it will be difficult to get a suitable partner. When a girl is
highly educated and she sees the different boys
coming to the house she may not like them. [22]

The number of unmarried females in India has always
been small; it is suggested here that highly educated urban
women may increasingly fall into this category, especially if
they refuse matches unsuitable, from their point of view. In

a brief article concerned with the fate of spinsters, I. Bhatnagar makes a similar observation:

> With the spread of female education women demand
> a choice in the matter [marriage]. Many of them
> would rather choose to remain a spinster than lead
> an unhappy life with a partner who is not up to
> them. A few of them inflict self-sacrifice on them-
> selves and refuse to be bound in wedlock because
> they find their parents cannot find a dowry for
> them or if they can, it will land them in an eco-
> nomic hardship for the lifetime.
>
> In middle class families parents in their anxiety
> to find a suitable match for their daughters wait
> too long till their girls cross the usual age limit,
> making their marriage a difficult proposition.
>
> . . . .
> Sometimes a woman is compelled to remain vir-
> gin to be able to support her family. The parents
> or relatives who compel a young woman to refrain
> from marriage for their own self-interest are de-
> serving of censure. The young woman is deeply
> wronged. [23]

Any statement about the level of education considered
desirable in an Indian wife should be qualified by specifying
the caste, religion, education, and economic circumstances
of the parties involved. Certainly for some rural Indians,
the high school graduate has already been ruined for marriage. For many urban educated men, the college graduate
is just about right. And for a few others, the college lecturer or doctor may make up in potential income what she
lacks in subservience.

As part of the small educated elite of India, do respondents feel that they have an obligation to others outside
the family circle? Or is education seen only as it affects
themselves? A loaded question, recognizably so, was asked
"Do you feel that you are expected to contribute to the society in any special ways because of your education?" Table
11 shows the distribution of explanations given by women
with different educational aspirations. Teaching and voluntary social service are named most frequently. Only those
who have advanced degrees or who hope to acquire them feel
that they can contribute in fields of work other than teaching
and they cite this more than one-fifth of the time.

TABLE 11 : OPINIONS OF EDUCATED WOMEN AS TO HOW THEY ARE EXPECTED TO
CONTRIBUTE TO SOCIETY

Ways in Which Society Expects Her to Contribute	Total		Those Who Expect Education to End with First Degree		Those Who Aspire to or have Advanced Degrees	
	No.	%	No.	%	No.	%
In general ways	16	16	5	18	11	15
Teaching	45	45	14	50	31	44
Social service	19	19	7	25	12	17
Household, family, children	4	4	2	8	2	3
Work, other than teaching	16	16			16	22
Total	100	100	28	101	72	101
No special ways	5		2		3	
Don't know	3		2		1	

*Table refers to number of times each way is mentioned. Some individuals gave multiple
answers. One respondent was not asked for this information and another did not give
educational plans. Thus, 95 respondents are represented in this table.

Another interesting finding is that contribution through one's own household, family or children is mentioned in only 4 per cent of the answers. Although many national leaders have stressed the importance of educating women in order that they become more enlightened mothers and wives, this idea is hardly reflected in these responses. Only 8 per cent of the sample say that they are not expected to contribute to society or don't know whether or not they are. Certainly the answers reflect some sentiment on the part of educated women that they are expected to use their knowledge in vocational fields, even though almost a fifth see the traditional charitable effort in social service as befitting their status.

Notes

1. India: A World in Transition, 2nd. ed. rev. (New York: Praeger, 1966), p. 159.

2. Marriage and Family in India, 3rd ed. rev. (Bombay: Oxford University Press, 1966), pp. 266-267.

3. Carl N. Degler, "Revolution Without Ideology: The Changing Place of Women in America," in R. J. Lifton, ed., The Woman in America (Boston: Beacon Press, 1964) p. 202.

4. It should be recalled that 29 per cent of the sample already held higher degrees when chosen. We shall consider as "less educated" those having only a B. A. or B. Sc. The "highly educated" or holders of higher degrees include those with master's, double bachelor's, medical or law degrees.

5. For Table 9, chi-square = 6. 961, d. f. = 2, the relationship being significant at the . 05 level. Dividing the sample differently, by projected educational attainment, we can group those who hold higher degrees with those now studying for them, and contrast them with those who hold only B. A. 's or B. Sc. 's and are not now studying. There is no statistically significant relationship between projected educational level and views about the role of education in marital choice. Nor is there a statistically significant relationship in terms of educational aspirations. However, it is interesting to note that all of the eight women who believe education to be a hindrance

in getting a mate fall within the group who now have
advanced degrees, are pursuing them, or hope to
pursue them. Of the 28 women with only one degree
who do not expect to study further, none views education as a hindrance.

6.   P. Thomas, Indian Women Through the Ages (Bombay:
     Asia Publishing House, 1964), pp. 315-316.

7.   A. S. Altekar, The Position of Women in Hindu Civili-
     zation, 3rd ed. (Delhi: Motilal Banarsidass, 1962),
     p. 62. The Sarda Act laid down 18 and 14 as the
     minimum legal age of marriage for boys and girls
     respectively.

8.   Early widowhood meant that the child-bride could never
     remarry and would suffer the indignities of a perma-
     nently stigmatized, childless, physically and socially
     deprived status.

9.   Wake Up India: A Plea for Social Reform (Adyar,
     Madras: Theosophical Publishing House, 1913),
     pp. 201-202.

10. Women and Social Injustice, (Ahmedabad: Navajivan
     Publishing House, 1942).

11. Immolation of widows. If the statement below by
     Margaret Cousins seems to stress the importance
     of women's freedom unduly, then note the one im-
     mediately following, which represents official gov-
     ernment thinking approximately 25 years later:

         No movement connected with the freedom of India
         seems more fundamental than the Freedom for
         Women's movement. Not all the Governments in
         the world can give India true Swaraj if Indians
         themselves, men and women, do not remove the
         chains of out-of-date custom that hold the higher-
         class Indian women in impoverishment of body,
         mind and soul. [Indian Womanhood Today, rev.
         ed. (Allahabad: Kitabistan, 1947; originally pub-
         lished in 1941), p. 45.]
         The Report of the Education Commission states:
         The significance of the education of girls cannot
         be overemphasized. For full development of our
         human resources, the improvement of homes and

for moulding the character of children during the
most impressionable years of infancy, the education
of women is of even greater importance than that
of men.   As stated earlier, the education of wom-
en can assist greatly in reducing the fertility rate.
In the modern world, the role of the woman goes
much beyond the home and the bringing up of children.   She is now adopting a career of her own
and sharing equally with men, the responsibility
for the development of the society in all its aspects.   This is the direction in which we shall
have to move.   In the struggle for freedom, Indian
women fought side by side with men.   This equal
partnership will have to continue in the fight against
hunger, poverty, ignorance and ill-health.   [Educa-
tion and National Development (New Delhi: Government of India Press, 1966), p.   135.]

12.   A. A. Khati, "Social Change in the Caste Hindu Family
      and its Possible Impact on Personality and Mental
      Health," Sociological Bulletin 12 (1963), pp. 146-
      163.   Margaret Cormack deals with the lack of sex
      education or preparation for marriage of Indian girls
      in The Hindu Woman (Bombay: Asia Publishing
      House, 1961; originally published by Teachers' Col-
      lege, Columbia University in 1953), pp. 109-112.
      One of the assistants was asked to summarize her
      reactions to this book.   On the topic of sex educa-
      tion, she wrote: "I agree with the author when she
      states that the complete lack of sex education is
      wrong and harmful.   Even to this day no sex edu-
      cation is given to girls at home."

13.   The Hindu Family in Its Urban Setting (Toronto:
      University of Toronto Press, 1961), p. 229.

14.   Rama Mehta, The Western Educated Hindu Woman (New
      York: Asia Publishing Company, 1970), p. 36.

15.   Marriage and Family in India, op. cit., p. 165.

16.   The Position of Women in Hindu Civilization, op. cit.,
      p. 328.

17.   G. S. Dutt, A Woman in India, (London: Hogarth
      Press, 1929).

18. Student Unrest in India, (Montreal: McGill-Queen's
        University Press, 1969), p. 181.

19. Ibid.

20. The Hindu Woman, op. cit., p. 49.

21. Student Unrest, op. cit., p. 187.

22. A few respondents made a point of saying that they did
        not feel a highly educated bridegroom was obligatory,
        but theirs was a minority viewpoint. Of course com-
        promises with this ideal may be made if the man has
        other outstanding qualifications.

23. "Spinsters," Social Welfare 11, no. 1 (April 1964): p.
        19.

Chapter IV

TRADITION AND CHANGE IN VIEWS OF MARRIAGE

The diffidence with which many respondents greeted questions about marriage has been mentioned. The professed indifference to this major event came as a surprise to one used to the extreme preoccupation of young western women with dating and mating. Literature on the formal aspects of arranged marriage did little to indicate that the remark "I have not thought about marriage" would be made by women in their middle twenties. However, as understanding of the Indian marriage system deepened, the fuller meaning which lay beneath this type of response became clearer.

Certain major norms and values which help define the Indian female's attitude toward marriage provided necessary clues. We have already discussed the notion of women's perpetual tutelage and dependence on men, the belief in her extreme sexuality, the idea of individual nature, and the importance of reputation, position and gossip. To these should be added consideration of the following significant, related features of Indian life: (1) the role of fatalism, religion and magic; (2) the compulsory nature of marriage and the problem of dowry; (3) the notions of duty and adjustment and the culturally prescribed duties of fathers and daughters; (4) the nature of family conflict and compromise; and (5) the use of third parties and indirection.

Many respondents, but especially the more conservative, evidence the belief in fate that is characteristic of their culture. While they may verbalize hopes about continuing their education, they take a much less active stance towards marriage, which is understood as an event which happens, and to which one must "adjust." This resignation to fate has been appropriate in the past, since marriage was, in effect, compulsory for women, and marital choice the problem of elders. The young woman may hear about parents' activities in searching for a mate for her almost by chance. Further, during the time of child marriage, the

young bride could not be expected to look forward to leaving
her home to live with strange in-laws. The bridge between
marriage and past roles has always been duty, and the
young bride, however unwilling, was expected to accept her
fate. The college graduate, who has been out in the world
and who hears and knows more about marriages, is probably
less able to keep her mind "blank" about it; yet that is the
culturally right thing. The traditional woman may internalize
this stance, making it difficult for her to develop a role in
marital choice if she is offered one. This was true of many
of the young Japanese studied by Robert Blood. Marriage
had been considered an inevitable occurrence which required
no judgment or intervention on their part. When these young
Japanese were given the right to choose their own mates,
many did not enjoy exercising it. [1]

Lack of involvement in the process of marital choice
does not mean that young people minimize the importance of
marriage. In fact, its very importance may be the reason
why they are not entrusted with freedom of choice and tend
to accept the judgment of their elders. Young Indian women
have much opportunity to learn about the proper behavior expected of the ideal Indian wife through stories, epics, and
anecdotes.

The father, then, has the awesome duty of selecting
life partners for his children, and may depend ultimately on
the matching of horoscopes, as well as the advice and help
of his wife and other family members. According to Altekar,
the practice of consulting horoscopes came into prominence
along with child marriage, thus providing support for the
father who had the duty of making fateful decisions for young
children. [2] The use of horoscopes was intended to minimize
risks, and continues to ease tension for some fathers. For
example, a father may be told by an astrologer that his
daughter is not fated to be married for some time, and
hence he need not begin the search for a husband. At
times, however, a very suitable union may be ruled out because the young peoples' horoscopes do not match. The
functions and dysfunctions of reliance on horoscopes could
profitably be studied.

Marriage had come to be regarded as obligatory for
girls by about 300 B. C., according to Altekar. [3] The norm
became so powerful at the beginning of the Christian era
that it resulted in various abuses. A daughter with some
obvious disability or disease might be married to some

highly undesirable person. According to Kapadia, the high cost of dowry in modern times still leads to unsuitable matches. [4]

Thomas maintains that a "commercial motive" in dowry developed during the later British period. A young man with a good education and good prospects became much sought after as a bridegroom, and parents of girls vied for the available prospects. "...[D]owry, in due course, became the deciding factor in the marriage market among several communities in India."[5]

In spite of the Dowry Prohibition Act of 1961, the practice continues, with doctors and engineers carrying the highest bounties. Since dowry, along with the high cost of marriages, is frequently condemned in print, it is surprising to find that 40 per cent of respondents answer "yes" when asked whether or not dowry is customary in their communities. [6] An approximately equal number maintain that it is not customary, with the remainder indicating that the practice varies within their communities. [7] Almost half of the married and engaged women say that it is not given in their communities, and they would be well-informed by their own experience. The prevalence of dowry may well be underestimated in these figures, both because the definition of dowry varies, and because it is disapproved of. A number of the husbands who are most favorably inclined toward their wife's employment did not accept dowry. It may be that the economic value of a working wife is now more clearly recognized and will become a substitute for dowry in the future. While a group of Mehta's respondents who were strongly opposed to dowry maintained that a good education was a substitute for it, they came from highly prestigious families who would not expect difficulties in finding bridegrooms. [8] This view was rarely verbalized by the respondents in the present study.

Unfortunately, a detailed analysis of the prevalence of dowry cannot be provided here. To do so would have required a sampling of parents, to whom the problem is most clear and most pressing. Occasionally parents would discuss the issue with us, and it was a frequent topic of criticism in academic circles. However, even those most opposed to the custom sometimes had to compromise by giving expensive gifts to the bridegroom and his family and by spending large sums of money on the weddings. The social pressures are such that parents may feel powerless to take a stand against dowry. Mehta's respondents discussed some of the dilemmas

involved and their own ambivalences. [9]   However, Kurian
maintains that there are some advantages to the dowry system:

> Dowry payments mean much financial strain, but
> have some positive aspects.   Girls have a chance
> of getting better partners when dowry is paid.   This
> smacks of commercialism but it is not so bad as it
> may seem at face-value when we consider the con-
> ditions under which they marry.   Arranged mar-
> riages are still the most prevalent form, and when
> there is a possibility of choice between two or three
> eligible girls, the boy might naturally choose one
> with some financial security as, in the absence of
> free choice, emotional ties have little meaning for
> him.
>   Dowry payment thus helps the girl to make the
> best match.   It also has a useful function when the
> girl is educated but not good-looking.   The attrac-
> tion of sufficient monetary compensation in the form
> of a dowry might tip the scale in her favour when
> the boy is not particular about looks.   Dowry thus
> forms a kind of social security and also makes up
> for property claims.   It is considered desirable
> for a girl to be married with a substantial sum as
> dowry, and, in addition to the obvious financial
> considerations, there are prestige points.   Girls
> who have no dowry are looked down upon by the
> family of the boy.   Sometimes this even affects
> those who marry for love. [10]

In spite of certain exceptions, and even with the dowry
system, the strong prescription favoring marriage led to a
situation in which there were virtually no unmarried adults
in traditional India. [11]   And, as has been mentioned, the 1961
Census figures indicate that even urban women are almost all
married by the time they reach age 34.

However, the growing economic independence of wom-
en, as well as changes in patterns of mate selection, may affect these rates in the future.   Levy has suggested that higher
education enables a girl to become aware of alternatives to
marriage. [12]

Educated women who rebel against the idea of dowry
are beginning to view the possibility of life-time careers.
One of the youngest respondents, already studying for her

master's degree in a scientific field, spoke most vehementl
against arranged marriage, as follows:

> The dowry is just like buying something on the
> market, just like selling goods. I won't go in for
> arranged marriage, no matter what. I think that
> if a girl marries her education will be wasted. I
> am not interested in marriage. I can do more fo
> the country if I am not married.

If it is the father's sacred duty to find a husband for
his daughter and to insure continuous male protection for he
after his death, what does this imply for the daughter's rol
She is certainly not primed to "fall in love." While "love
marriage" is a frequently used concept, falling in love is
considered an accident rather than the active seeking out of
a mate. The anxiety of finding husbands is traditionally tha
of the father. Thus Ross can write, with some justification

> It could be argued that Hindu girls have one great
> advantage over western girls in college in that, as
> their marriages are still arranged by their parent
> they do not have to worry about finding husbands
> themselves during their college years; whereas
> girls in western colleges are often faced with two
> of the most difficult tasks of their lives at the
> same time--that of finding a husband and preparing
> themselves for future careers. [13]

What if the young woman is concerned about her mar
riage or is afraid that it might not come to pass? To ques
tion her father would be indelicate, might intimate that he i
not doing his duty, and might reflect interest in sexual mat
ters. The following episode illustrates:

A single Christian woman, 25 years of age, was inte
viewed by the author and a Christian assistant. Because th
respondent's shyness and apparent embarrassment might hav
been due to the author's presence, two assistants were sent
back for further informal conversation. Their encounter
with an angry father is described below:

> The father told us that the interviewee was much
> upset because of the interview carried out on her
> on the 27th. He said that questions on marriage
> should not be discussed with an unmarried and in-
> experienced girl as it would spoil her mind and be-

sides that, she would not know anything about marriage. He seemed to be a very religious-minded
person and said that we cannot decide anything
about marriage, as everything takes place according to God's will. He even quoted certain lines
from the Bible. I tried to convince him that whatever we take down will be kept confidential and
will not be revealed to anyone. He still insisted
that he doesn't mind us asking her anything, but
questions on <u>marriage</u> should <u>not</u> be asked, as he
himself knows that her mind is blank on this subject and that she is very innocent and can't answer
such questions.

For this daughter to admit that she had thought about marriage would have been a confession of evil thoughts and lack
of innocence.

The traditional attitude of the young woman is probably well-expressed by the respondent who, when asked if her
future plans included marriage, replied, "That is the father's
duty. I can adjust." Marriage has been considered necessary in order for a woman to achieve her highest place and
insure her security. Tales of the unfortunate fate of spinster
relatives might help a girl to understand this, and prepare
her for the inevitable.

"Adjustment," the woman's duty, is used very broadly
to refer to any situation in which a woman is placed in a
new, different or disagreeable position. Thus, if the parents
refuse to allow her to work, she adjusts; if she goes to live
with orthodox in-laws, she adjusts to their ways. In doing
so, the woman adopts rationalizations which help her to accept her fate. Adjustment also takes the form of a highly
developed sensitivity to the needs and wishes of others. The
most artful women become masterful at manipulation, learning to wait for the proper time, circumstances and issues on
which they can express their own viewpoints. Once married,
the young bride is expected to look up to her husband as lord
and master, anticipate his "will and wish" and cater to his
needs. Her obligations to her in-laws are very strong, as
they have been to elders in her own family. In effect, she
practices the same arts of adjustment that she has previously
learned, but does not have the advantage of doing so with
people very familiar to her.

Open conflict within the Indian family is feared and

disapproved; and youth hesitate to hurt parents or in-laws.
One finds the hope that, within the family, discussion will
lead to compromise or to convincing one member of another
position.   Even those who admitted to open disagreements
with parents expressed the wish not to hurt them.   A very
outspoken non-Brahmin Hindu, studying for her M. A., said
that she planned to marry out of her caste if that should be
necessary in order to get an educated mate.   As an after-
thought, she added, "Sometimes I think I should try to please
my father because the others [sisters] didn't."   This concern
for parents above oneself was revealed many times.

Ross' findings are similar.   In her study of student
indiscipline, she tried to ascertain the extent of family disagreement and conflict.   She found that while most of the
college students in her sample disagreed with their parents
on some points, they "did not dare reveal their feelings because they could not face family displeasure."[14]   Of the 91
women students in her sample, 32 admitted to quarrelling
with mothers but only 14 to quarrels with fathers.   Ross
concludes:

> Quarrels at home are kept to a minimum in many
> of the families because the children either respect
> their parents and do not want to hurt or challenge
> them, or have not the courage to express their
> own views. [15]

When family discussion develops around an issue on
which there is disagreement, the opinions of various family
members may be sought.   A woman with the prestige and
self-confidence inspired by a college degree is more likely
than a less-educated daughter to feel bold enough to enter
into such talks with elders.   Thus, we may expect a change
in the educated woman's position of influence within the family without necessarily anticipating the sharp and open conflic
characteristic of some other cultures.   Within the in-law
family, of course, she will have to respond more carefully
and show that she knows her place.

Neighbors, relatives, and friends, as well as professional matchmakers may be involved in arranging marriages
One of the consequences of the use of third parties is the
opportunity to influence people without their knowing the ultimate source.   Thus even when the concerned individuals
seem to be passive in their own marriage arrangements,
they may be playing a role.   Since third parties can be ap-

proached to suggest particular matches, the percentage of "love marriages" may be higher than is apparent. The use of go-betweens may prove a helpful mechanism in the transition between arranged marriage and the probably increasing number of self-selected mates.

Seen within the cultural imperatives discussed above, a number of answers to questions about marriage made more sense. Variations in response often reflected an individual's traditionalism. Having made the proper modest show of disinterest in marriage, most women would go on to discuss such questions as the role of education in affecting marital chances and in adjusting to marriage, the proper age at which they thought a woman should marry, and whether or not they believed a girl could live a happy life without marriage. A few of the more traditional were unable or unwilling to elaborate much in their answers; others went on to tell anecdotes about various women of their acquaintance.

In contrast to the others, the nine women who maintained that they did not intend to marry volunteered this information almost as soon as the subject of marriage came up. They took an active stance toward their own fate and often claimed that their will would prevail. These cases will be discussed in greater detail later in the chapter.

Let us look now at some of the views expressed in response to a number of questions about marriage.

To get respondents' viewpoints about the possibility of life without marriage, we asked, "Do you feel that a girl who does not marry can lead a happy life or that she cannot?[16] Fewer than half of the 95 responding said that she could not. More than a third were unequivocal in their position that a woman could be happy without marriage, while an additional 17 per cent believed that she could be happy under the proper circumstances. Thus, a large proportion of these educated women do not accept the dictum that marriage is essential. Furthermore, in explaining their positions few hold that marriage is a matter of duty. Their reasoning will be explained shortly.

Breaking down the sample by projected educational attainment and marital status produces interesting contrasts (Table 12). Those women who hold advanced degrees are grouped with the ones currently studying for a second or third degree, and are contrasted with the ones who hold one

bachelor's degree and are not now studying.   About three-
fifths of the first, more educated group maintain that a woman can or sometimes can, be happy without marriage, while
only about two-fifths of the less educated do so. [17]   However,
this difference is not statistically significant, and the possibility of a relationship should be studied further.

TABLE 12: OPINIONS ABOUT A WOMAN'S HAPPINESS WITH-
OUT MARRIAGE, BY EDUCATION AND MARITAL STATUS

| | Can a girl who does not marry lead a happy life? | | | |
Status	Total	No	Yes	Sometimes
Projected Education				
Higher degree				
number	55	21	22	12
percent	100	38	40	22
B. A. or B. Sc.				
number	40	23	13	4
percent	101	58	33	10
Marital Status				
Single				
number	76	31	31	14
percent	100	41	41	18
Married				
number	19	14	3	2
per cent	10	74	16	11

It has been suggested that higher education enables a
woman to become aware of the alternatives to marriage.
That of work is only now becoming a reality for middle class
Indian women.   Of course, the women with advanced degrees
have better career possibilities than those holding only a
bachelor's degree.

However, the view that one can be happy without marriage may also represent anticipatory socialization to the
spinster role.   At least some individuals may be beginning
to adjust--their expected way of meeting fate--to future possibilities.   As indicated earlier, while they have acquired, in

some ways, more varied life alternatives, the more highly educated women are apt to have decreased their chances of marriage. When the condition of advanced education is added to the traditional requirements such as caste endogamy and matching horoscopes, it drastically limits the circle of potential bridegrooms. That pattern found by Levy in modern China, in which highly educated women preferred spinsterhood to unsuitable marriages, may well repeat itself in India.

Not surprisingly, married respondents tend to support the desirability of their own status. Almost three-quarters of them, in contrast to only 41 per cent of the single ones, take the position that marriage is essential to woman's happiness. [18] While adjustment to fate again appears to be playing a role, the lack of unanimity shows that answers are not wholly related to the individual's own status. We find no apparent relationship between age and point of view about the necessity of marriage.

In explaining their position, those who feel that women cannot be happy without marriage clearly refer to some of the traditional notions we have discussed. Three types of reasons are mentioned, related to the problem of protection and living arrangements, biological or companionship needs, and social pressures and criticisms.

The need for protection is the reason most frequently mentioned by those who feel marriage is essential, totalling almost 30 per cent of the responses. The following comment is typical in its suggestion that marriage is most important after the "girl" has reached 35 or 40 years of age: "Up to 40 years a girl can be happy without marriage. But after that age she feels the need of somebody to look after her. If she is married she can have children to look after her."

Others point out that the need for a husband is greatest "when the father and mother are no longer there," rather than for the particular relationship a wife may share with her spouse. The need for protection usually requires that a woman live with her brother after the parents' death. While brother and sister relationships may be warm during childhood, adult brothers and their wives do not enjoy a good reputation for hospitality. A Brahmin studying for her doctor's degree sums up the situation in this way:

Under the present Indian set-up of society, I feel
an unmarried girl may not lead a happy life. Mere
money may not bring happiness as her social environment is not very cheerful for her. While the
parents are alive it is all right. But then she
will have to live with her brother, and the brother's
wife may not treat her right. She can't live with
her sisters because they are not in their own
homes. It's very difficult for unmarried girls living away from home. We have several hostels for
working women, but it is not so nice for them.

While the need for companionship, another reason
given for marrying, may be thought of as an emotional need,
it is very real in its most literal sense. A non-Brahmin
Hindu M.A., moving into her late twenties, spells out what
lack of a companion means:

It is difficult to be a spinster. Only to some extent can she be happy. She has to spend the
whole day alone, unless in a family.... Also, a
girl in India, even if highly educated, can't go out
to the cinema or anywhere. That makes it difficult. She must always have someone.

Although some respondents complain about the continuing requirement of chaperonage, none say they would choose to
violate this convention. We have already pointed out that
travelling alone may make the young woman a target for
teasing or abuse. Thus the need for male protection, as a
self-fulfilling prophecy, persists. As a parallel, perhaps,
modern American cities are increasingly considered "unsafe"
for unaccompanied females, especially at night, so that
travelling in groups or in male company becomes an informal practice, corresponding in actuality to Bangalore's
formal norm.

The belief that most women have strong sexual needs
or instincts continues to prevail, even though some women
feel that these needs can be controlled. More than a quarter of the responses describing why marriage is essential
refer to a need for sexual relations or a maternal instinct.
While the point is more often made with some delicacy, the
following exposition by a married respondent is very direct:
"She cannot [be happy]. No man or woman is complete until she or he marries. There is a natural biological urge
for everyone." A very religious Christian expresses her-

self in this way:

> A girl who does not marry can lead a happy life
> only if she is a spiritual-minded person not at-
> tached with carnal pleasures. ...   [S]he needs
> some special call from God to be like that.   Other-
> wise she will like to marry.

A more extreme view of this need is expressed in
Social Welfare, an Indian journal very much concerned with
advancing the cause of women:

> The unmarried woman has emotional needs which
> have to be satisfied.   One of them is the hunger
> for motherhood.   The decision to remain unmar-
> ried for life is not good, as a rule, for the men-
> tal health of a woman.   Love is a woman's whole
> existence.   It dominates a woman's life. [19]

References to criticism and social pressures are
made by a surprisingly small proportion of respondents (18
per cent).   One woman believes that a girl should marry,
if only to prevent her parents from being criticized.   But
others indicate that the woman herself may not have an
easy time.   A young mother describes the plight of an unmarried woman in this way: "In the case of a joint family,
she is all the time nagged at and she is not left in peace."
An unmarried Brahmin claims: "If one is not married, she
has to face the rubbish comments from society." While it
appears that societal pressures on the unmarried woman are
lessening, traditional living arrangements and the needs for
protection and companionship still present practical difficulties.

Those respondents who feel marriage is not essential
to happiness demonstrate how the role of spinster is becoming legitimitized.   The reason mentioned most frequently,
totalling one-quarter of the responses, is that there are
satisfactory alternatives to marriage.   This not only takes
cognizance of new opportunities but also fulfills the past requirement that women be kept busy.   Suitable careers as
well as social service work are mentioned as ways of doing
so.   An unmarried Moslem in her late twenties claims that
a girl can adjust to being unmarried if she is occupied:
"An unmarried girl can lead a happy life provided she is
employed, because she will be occupied, independent, and
have no time to brood over it." However, a young Brah-

min shows a much more positive evaluation of single life:
"Yes, a girl who does not marry can lead a happy life.
She need not worry about family and all.   And she can work
more for the country rather than for her own self. "

The untraditional viewpoint that an unmarried woman
may be independent best illustrates change in role conceptions and is mentioned in fully one-fifth of the explanations.
The term "independence" usually refers to financial independence, but sometimes also to independence from ties of
marriage and family responsibilities, as in the last statement above.   Financial independence implies that the woman
is no longer dependent on the family for funds, though she
may indeed contribute to it.   Her economic role will be
recognized in increased status within the family, even though
her salary may be turned over to the male head of the
house.   For some women, the independence attached to remaining single means one will not have to cater to the wishes of a husband.   As such, it makes rebellion against existing role definitions explicit.

The notion of independence does not appear to include
the premise that independent living arrangements are possibl
Respondents who say that a woman need not marry tend to
minimize the problems of companionship and security.   Few
of them mention the need for a proper home environment,
so prominent in arguments of women who feel marriage is
essential.   The avoidance of this issue suggests that living
arrangements for the unmarried are not considered ideal
even by the group who feel a single life is possible.

Twenty-one per cent of the answers refer to the particular qualities or "nature" of the woman.   Among qualities
spelled out are: having will power, being adjustable, being
spiritually-minded, and not "liking marriage" or not being
suited to marriage.   Will-power enables one to resist sexua
temptation or to overcome social disapproval.   Adjustability
is considered necessary for a home situation in which one
never takes on the wife role, and remains subordinate to
other females.   A woman who has been earning for a long
while or who has an engrossing career may be considered
less suited to running a household.   Here we see that the
accepted belief in differences in nature permits some diver-
gence from the rule that girls should be married.

While not all take the position with equal vigor, the
nine women who maintain that they will not marry are pub-

licly proclaiming themselves as deviants from cultural expectations. They define their nature as not suited to the
marriage role and imply that, as a consequence, the parents'
wishes will not predominate. Some of them say that their
parents will respect their feelings, which suggests that such
an understanding may already exist. By stating openly that
they do not wish to marry, these women temper society's
speculation that something is wrong with the family or that
the father is not fulfilling his duty. This stance is clearly
different from that of women who claim not to have thought
about marriage; they have thought about it and rejected it.

In some cases it may have been taken for granted
that because of an early illness or disability, the woman was
not destined for marriage. One individual indicated that she
had grown up accustomed to the idea that she, among her
sisters, would never marry. Another, a nineteen year old,
whose family is well off, appeared to be somewhat sickly.
She volunteered the following: "I have decided not to marry.
My sisters--they will be happy married. [But what if your
parents want you to?] No, they will do as I say. They
will agree with me."

An educated woman who is helping to support her
family may be well aware that her earnings are needed, as
illustrated by the case of a 30-year-old Brahmin. She is
described by the interviewer as follows:

> She is working because of the financial difficulties.
> She is still unmarried. As such she doesn't think
> of marriage at all. She feels very strongly that
> a girl can be happy without marriage. They do
> not have to bother. Neither children nor family
> conflicts. She says that she is not intending to
> marry.... She was frank about the family income
> and told me it is necessary for her to work to bal-
> ance the family expenditures.

That some women lack enthusiasm for marriage must
also be considered in view of Theodorson's findings about
cross-national variations in eagerness to marry. Comparing
Indians, Burmese, and Chinese in Singapore, he points out
that in all three cultures motivation to marry was traditionally supported by strong sanctions. Finding what he considers a large percentage of female college students who express a desire not to marry, Theodorson concludes that
there has been a decline in the strength of traditional mo-

tivations for marriage.   Comparing the three cultures, Indian women proved to be the most averse to marriage, with
28 per cent of them answering that they would not like to
marry if it were up to them. [20]

In discussing the necessity of marriage, a number of
our respondents point out that marriage itself does not insure happiness.   A single Brahmin studying for her M. Sc.
had this explanation:

> An unmarried girl can certainly lead a happy life.
> Highly qualified girls are sometimes incapable of
> adjustment.   Marriage is not necessary for a hap-
> py life.   Many marriages are unsatisfactory and
> independence is preferable to an unhappy marriage.

Others mention such possibilities as early widowhood,
forced marriages, difficult husbands, or orthodox in-laws.
Thus, the point is made that chances of unhappiness are
present in either case, whether one marries or remains
single.

Kurian, in his study of married Syrian Christians
from the State of Kerala, describes four patterns of marital
choice, as follows: marriage which is (1) arranged according to the ideas of the parents; (2) arranged by the parents
with the consent of the respondent; (3) the respondent's own
choice with the consent of the parents; and (4) the respondent's own choice without the consent of the parents. [21]   The
second pattern was most frequent among both his urban and
rural respondents.   Members of our sample also consider
this pattern most prevalent, but perceive education as providing the woman more influence.   A small proportion see
education or employment as enabling a young woman to
choose her own mate.

While opinions about the prevailing marriage system
were not sought directly, several questions elicited assumptions about it.   Among these were the questions of whether
education and employment help or hinder a girl in finding a
suitable marriage partner.

Respondents often cite the continuing existence of arranged marriage to clarify other answers.   For example, a
married Moslem states:

> I think education helps a girl to find a suitable
> partner, but here in India 75 per cent of the

parents arrange a match, and it is for them to decide what and who is suitable for their daughter.

Remarks referring to the second pattern named by Kurian were more frequent. A single Brahmin maintains, "Employment helps a girl in contact with different men, and she learns what type of man would suit her best. The partners are still chosen by parents, for the girl's inspection."

Respondents were asked how education aids in mate selection. The reasons given most frequently imply that a degree is an asset in the traditional marriage market. Thus, 46 per cent of the responses hold that some men or their parents prefer graduates for wives. More than a third of the responses reflect the belief that the educated woman has increased influence on her parents' selection, reasoning that education makes a woman more knowledgeable about men and more willing to express her opinions about them. While 9 per cent of the respondents go so far as to suggest that educated women may select their own mates, they would not necessarily condone such action without parental approval. Judging from the tone of the total interviews, these college-educated women rarely consider acting against the expressed wishes of their parents. The bolder ones persist longer in attempting to convince parents to accept their viewpoints.

TABLE 13: COMPARISON OF THE EFFECTS OF EDUCATION AND EMPLOYMENT ON MARITAL CHANCES

	Education		Employment	
	No.	%	No.	%
Helps	60	63	36	39
Hinders	8	8	22	24
Neither; or, sometimes helps, sometimes hinders	27	28	35	38
Total	95	99	93	101

Comparing the assessment of the effects of education and employment, respectively, on marital chances (Table 13), we see that education is definitely viewed more positively. Sixty-three per cent of respondents say that education helps in finding a mate, but only 39 per cent feel this is true of

employment.[22]   Table 13 shows that over a third of the respondents believe that the effect of employment on marital
chances varies--that it sometimes helps and sometimes hinders, or that it may do neither.   This viewpoint reflects a
changing situation in which employment, once stigmatized
for middle class women, is gaining in legitimacy.   Chapter
V deals at length with the question of the respectability of
work.

Although employment is considered to be less helpful
than education, the reasoning again suggests presuppositions
about arranged marriage.   Interpreting various explanations
(Table 14), one notes that employment may be viewed as an
asset in the traditional marriage market or alternately as
providing more opportunity to enter into choice of mate.
Thus, the statement, "an employed girl can help her husband

TABLE 14: HOW EMPLOYMENT HELPS IN FINDING A PARTNER

		Responses	
		No.	%
1.	Girl can help boy economically	24	38
2.	Girl may choose own partner	11	17
3.	Boys like employed girls	9	14
4.	Some boys' families like employed girls	5	8
5.	Girl has more knowledge of people and desirable traits	5	8
6.	Girl is known and seen by more people	4	6
7.	Girl has more to say in influencing parents' choice	1	2
8.	Other	2	3
9.	Believe it helps but no reason given	3	5
	Total	64	101

economically" means that her value to the prospective family is enhanced.   The statement, "she can get to know more
people" suggests greater opportunity to use her own judgment.   A Brahmin lecturer implies that employed women
will make better use of their veto power over the parents'

choice. She maintains, "Employment helps a girl in contact with different men, and she learns what type of man would suit her best. The partners are still chosen by parents, for the girl's inspection." And a Hindu stenographer, of a non-Brahmin community, shows how traditional patterns of mate selection can be modified: "When in employment she can meet people. Some third person who comes to know about this may tell the parents, and it can be arranged thus."

Knowledge about a potential bride, and her availability is of some importance. The working woman will be known and seen by more people. Eleven women say that an employed girl can choose her own partner. Thus we can observe the nascent belief that education and employment may be used to modify patterns of marital choice.

Furthermore, these explanations illustrate the ways in which the transition from arranged marriage toward marriage by choice may take place. The educated woman feels that she is in a better position to judge the candidates presented by her parents than she would be if she were uneducated. Hence, even before structural facilities are available for individual choice (e.g., an approved dating system), the woman has started to develop criteria relevant for mate selection. At first she may use much the same standards as her elders, as does this lively young Brahmin clerical worker. Only in her last sentence does she indicate any concern with personal qualities:

> An uneducated girl knows nothing of the world, will just take whom her parents say, whatever they tell her--'he's a graduate,' 'he is well-settled,' she'll accept. But the educated girl knows much more and can choose better. She knows which degrees are better. I wouldn't want to marry a lawyer, for instance. These fellows have to work very hard. Or a doctor. They have to sacrifice some of their desires. A lawyer will make so much this month, a different amount next month. And a medical practitioner, too. But an engineer, he will make a fixed amount and have fixed hours. If they tell me an Arts graduate, I will know it's not so good as a Science graduate. We will be meeting various boys and seeing how they act, and we can judge.

While educated women claim a potentially greater role
in the selection of their mates, their exercise of this option
is still to be demonstrated. Some single women may be
preparing themselves psychologically to exercise their veto,
but there was no case reported where any one had turned
down a potential bridegroom. This undoubtedly occurs at
times, but its frequency is unknown. A number of married
women indicate that they acquiesced readily in their parents'
choice, as in the following case:

> Education helps the girl to have a frank talk with
> the future partner and parents. An uneducated
> girl will not have the courage to go and talk to
> her parents about her future. In many cases the
> educated girl can talk. Frankly though, I didn't.
> My parents would never do anything to harm me.
> They would look into everything carefully. And so
> far they have not done wrong by me.

As has already been suggested, the use of third parties provides a bridge toward greater participation in selection by the couples involved. It was indicated that, under
the usual system, a woman who is known and seen by many
people becomes more prominent as a marital possibility.
A young Moslem maintains that "even" among members of
her religious group some girls are able to "find husbands
through working."[23] She explains that an inquiry about her
sister had come through a contact made at the latter's place
of employment. In this case, the family happened not to
agree to the match. But, in addition, young people may become acquainted with each other at work. Earlier a respondent's remarks were quoted in which she observed that
third parties might be utilized to arrange a match desired
by the couple involved. While other methods operate informally, the appearance of an arranged marriage is still
considered good form. This is implied in the statement of
a Christian graduate student, who asserts that some marriages are arranged "in name only."

The acceptance of an economic role for educated
women is reflected in answers which suggest that they may
be considered an asset by prospective in-law families. Of
those who view employment positively, more than half stress
the fact that an employed woman can help her mate financially. Perhaps even more revealing is the fact that the
vast majority of respondents believe that a mother may work
if her earnings are needed. Almost one-third of our mar-

ried respondents were working at the time of the interview, while others were seeking work.

The economic role of the potential bride may eventually take the place of dowry. Comparing the reported family practice with regard to dowry of women who are working or seeking work with those who are either at home or studying for higher degrees, we find a significant difference. Those who are employed or seeking employment are much more likely to report that their families do not expect to give or receive dowry (Table 15). [24] A more thorough study of dowry practices might test this correlation.

TABLE 15: DOWRY PRACTICES BY EMPLOYMENT STATUS OF WOMEN

	Whether Family Accepts Dowry*							
Status	Total		Yes		Sometimes		No	
	No.	%	No.	%	No.	%	No.	%
Employed; seeking work	51	54	13	34	9	56	29	73
In school/home	43	46	25	66	7	44	11	28
Total	94	100	38	100	16	100	40	101

*"Accepts dowry" means the family expects to give a dowry.

According to various sacred texts, the daughter in a family lacking a male heir might be declared an appointed daughter and take the place of a son in performing religious duties. The marriageability of this substitute son ("Putrika") was sometimes held in question. [25] Similarly, it seems that a highly educated daughter may now be considered eligible to take the son's place in helping to support parents and younger siblings. Under present circumstances, an employed daughter is no longer able to help her parents once she gets married, but is expected to give her salary to her husband. Hence, her marriage may be postponed indefinitely.

Ross also refers to this new economic role of middle class women in The Hindu Family in Its Urban Setting, describing in detail a case in which a young woman gave up the prospect of marriage so that she could help her family financially. 26 The same investigator found the economic role of women to be even more pronounced in her later studies. 27 Of the employed women in our sample, 77 per cent were giving more than half of their earnings to their families.

In order to see whether educated women expect to have special problems of adjustment, we asked, "What are the major adjustments an educated woman will have to make in marriage?" For some, the simple answer, "She will have to adjust to everything," seems enough. Many answer the question in terms of the group to which the woman will have to adjust. Twenty per cent mention the need to adjust only to in-laws; 15 per cent only to the husband, and 18 per cent specify the need to adjust to both the husband and his family members. Other modifications of behavior named are: the need to adjust to the customs or environment of the new family, the need to change some aspect of one's personality or ideas, and economic adjustments. Married respondents tend to be much more specific than the single ones. A 22-year-old married Brahmin explains her understanding of required behavior as follows:

> She has to intelligently show to the parents-in-law, if it is a joint family, that their way of life suits her, in spite of minor differences.... Education helps in the sense that one can have a better unde standing of the problems.... The way my parents brought me up also helped. They told me to show the family that I like them and that in time I would become one with them. From education I know that I should not oppose them on important things. I will not voice my objections and I will get over it.... It is much easier to adjust to one person than to the joint family. I think it is even harder for the man--he has to please his parents and to please his wife. It's much easier if they are living separately.

A 21-year-old married Christian explains her adjustments thus:

> My husband's family is not very educated. So with them I have to be simple. It means not act like I am more educated than them. But

> since I am not living with them, there is no prob-
> lem to adjust. Education helps in making these
> adjustments. [An educated girl] will be more cul-
> tured. A less educated girl might fight but an edu-
> cated girl will not like to fight.

Fully 85 per cent of the sample believe that education helps
in adjusting to marriage. Only 5 per cent believe that it
hinders, with the remainder saying that education sometimes
helps and sometimes hinders. Over 60 per cent of the reasons given in explanation describe the educated woman as
more understanding and more broad-minded. The related
reason, that an educated woman will have learned to mix
with different kinds of people, received 16 per cent of the
mentions. An equal percentage of answers stress the various types of helpful knowledge than an educated woman can
bring to marriage.

Education is viewed as making a woman more rather
than less adaptable to her role in the new family. Clearly,
respondents feel that education will not cause them to chal-
lenge the traditional expectations of obedience to husbands
and in-laws, but will enable them to handle role requirements better. In a sense, these young women are describing the expected consequences of culture contact in replacing
the past isolation and seclusion of women. The educated
woman is pictured as being more understanding, more knowledgeable, more open-minded, and more "cultured" in dealing
with people--provided she is careful not to act self-important
because of her education. The respondents imply that past
generations of brides have not, in practice, been entirely
able to accept their role prescriptions. Despite what she
has been taught about adjusting, the uneducated bride finds
it difficult to accept the ideas and customs of the new family
if these vary from what she has known all her life. Furthermore, because of a lack of social contact outside the family,
she is ill at ease and less graceful in relating to her new
family.

The few women who feel that education neither helps
nor hinders marital adjustment stress the individual qualities
of the bride, as exemplified in this statement by a married
non-Brahmin Hindu:

> She cannot behave as she likes after marriage.
> Education in the broad sense helps to make adjust-
> ments. Sometimes uneducated people can adjust

better than the educated. It is not graduation that
helps or hinders, but the understanding or the
sense of judging what is right and wrong.

The dilemmas of the modern educated woman in adjusting to
the traditional wifely role are recognized, but the notion of
obedience is not rejected in this thoughtful response, written
by a woman now studying for an advanced degree in another
city:

> Educated women are old enough to have decided
> opinions. She will have to adjust herself to the
> husband deciding for her. ... Education is pri-
> marily a hindrance. But, if given second place
> in her life it is bound to be a help since it cul-
> tivates her mind and she will pass on the message
> of education .... Many men expect their wives
> to help in bringing additional income to the family.
> But they never help her in the household work. It
> is impossible for a girl to manage both single-
> handedly. In effect, she will have to strike a
> bargain of mutual help with him.
>   When an educated girl of modern outlook is mar-
> ried into a family following old traditions, the
> problem of adjustment is severe. She finds it
> hard to keep her independent spirit under control
> and remember that her husband's word is law.
> Though education becomes the main reason for
> the appearance of problems, it again helps in find-
> ing an answer to the problems.

A few respondents assert that an educated woman is
able to modify the traditional role of wife. While this
young Christian woman, studying for a second degree,
maintains that education helps in adjustment, her explanation is deviant in that it stresses a more independent posture
"The educated girl knows how to behave but she has some
independence of mind. She doesn't have to be a doormat.
She can think for herself and doesn't have to agree to every
thing. "

Even though it is claimed that an educated woman will
be able to adjust well to the usual role of wife, she may not
have to play this role in exactly the traditional way. The
in-laws may be unable to ignore her education so easily.
They may come to share the pride that many parents take
in their highly-educated daughters, and accord the educated

daughter-in-law a somewhat higher family status.   One
should also note that some of the expectations voiced by
single women are not based in real experience, but on
their idealized conceptions of the wifely role.

Expectations of the unmarried women tend to include
the prospect of going to live in a joint family, but chances
appear more than even that those who marry will eventually
be in their own households.   Thirteen of the 19 married respondents are now living in nuclear households.   To many
respondents, the problem of adjusting to a husband seems
relatively miniscule compared to the adjustments required in
an in-law joint family.   However, one may hypothesize that
as the nuclear family becomes more common, husband-wife
role expectations will undergo some revision.   In the process
this relationship is likely to become more closely scrutinized
and possibly redefined.

The trend of preference for later age at marriage,
noted by other observers, is confirmed by our data.

In answer to the question, "At what age do you think
a girl should get married?" the median approved range is
from 21 to 24 years of age.   The most frequently chosen
lower and upper limits are 20 and 25.   Thirteen per cent
of respondents suggest a preferred upper limit over age 25,
indicating that the acceptable age for marriage may be extended even further.   Of the ten respondents who are over
25 years of age, seven are still unmarried.

Married women differ from single ones on the issue
of the appropriate age at marriage.   Their median preferred
range is from 20 to 21 while that of single women is from
21 to 24.   The more highly educated respondents envision a
wider age range than do the less educated, suggesting average limits of 20 to 24 as contrasted with 21 to 23 named by
the latter.

The age of each of the single women was compared
with the range that she considered suitable for marriage.   Of
the 76 single women who answered this question, 35 per cent
had not reached their preferred minimum, 47 per cent were
within the preferred range, and 17 per cent were past the
age they considered best for marriage (percentages rounded).
It is interesting to note that this last percentage, based on
their own views, is considerably larger than the 10 per cent
who are past the modal upper limit of 25 years of age.

Notes

1. Robert O. Blood, Jr., Love Match and Arranged
    Marriage (Glencoe, N.Y.: The Free Press, 1967),
    ch. 1.

2. A. S. Altekar, The Position of Women in Hindu Civili-
    zation, 3rd ed. (Delhi: Motilal Banarsidass, 1962),
    p. 72.

3. Ibid., p. 32.

4. K. M. Kapadia, Marriage and Family in India, 3rd ed.
    rev. (Bombay: Oxford University Press, 1966), p.
    137.

5. P. Thomas, Indian Women Through the Ages (Bombay:
    Asia Publishing House, 1964), p. 372.

6. See Kapadia, op. cit., p. 137; Swarn Hooja, "Dowry
    System Among the Hindus in North India: A Case
    Study," Indian Journal of Social Work 28, no. 4
    (January 1968): 411-426; Vimal Balasubrahmanyan,
    "Wedding Southern Style," Caravan, The Fortnightly
    of National Resurgence, no. 343 (August 15, 1966):
    17-18.

7. In his study of marriage among Kerala Christian Indi-
    ans, Kurian found that 44 out of 60 urban men, as
    contrasted with 59 out of 65 rural men, had accepted
    dowry at the time of marriage. George Kurian, The
    Indian Family in Transition: A Case Study of Ker-
    ala Syrian Christians (The Hague: Mouton and Co.,
    1961), p. 76.

8. Rama Mehta, The Western Educated Hindu Woman (New
    York: The Asia Pub. Co., 1970), p. 133.

9. Ibid., pp. 131-134.

10. Kurian, op. cit., p. 121.

11. William J. Goode, World Revolution and Family Pat-
    terns (Glencoe, N.Y.: The Free Press, 1963), p.
    236.

12. In describing changes that have taken place in modern

China, he states, "Save for religious virtuoso[s], the 'traditional' Chinese society was almost completely devoid of unmarried adults, either male or female, save in those extreme economic straights when a man could not secure a wife. Neither bachelor nor 'old maid' had any place in the society. The new ways changed this. Careers other than marriage were now open to women, and some women chose to follow them rather than to marry. Unmarried women in professional or worker roles are an increasingly common sight in China, and the marriage age of many other women is being postponed until much later in life than would have been possible in 'traditional' China. Some women remain unmarried because they will not accept a marriage arranged by their parents and cannot arrange a suitable one themselves." [Marion J. Levy, Jr., The Family Revolution in Modern China (Cambridge: Harvard University Press, 1949), p. 301.]

13. Aileen D. Ross, The Hindu Family in Its Urban Setting (Toronto: University of Toronto Press, 1961), p. 321.

14. Aileen D. Ross, Student Unrest in India (Montreal: McGill-Queen's University Press, 1969), pp. 141-142.

15. Ibid., p. 142.

16. Women tend to call themselves girls, perpetually. Even though the respondents' own terminology, "girl," was used in the interviews, the term "woman" has been adopted as more appropriate for our own discussion.

7. If we break down education another way, by degree of education already attained, we find no significant difference between the attitudes of the two groups on this question, and very similar percentage distributions.

8. Chi-square = 6.761, d.f. = 2. The relationship is significant at the .05 level.

9. I. Bhatnagar, "Spinsters," Social Welfare 11, no. 1 (April 1964): p. 19.

20. George A. Theodorson, "Cross-National Variations in Eagerness to Marry, " in H. K. Geiger, ed. , <u>Comparative Perspectives on Marriage and the Family</u> (Boston: Little, Brown and Co. , 1968), p. 131.

21. Kurian, <u>op. cit.</u> , p. 67.

22. For Table 13, chi-square = 12. 609, d. f. = 2, and the difference is significant at the . 01 level.

23. Moslems are generally considered to be more conservative than other groups in family matters.

24. For Table 15, chi-square = 11. 762, d. f. = 2, which is significant at the . 01 level.

25. Shakuntala Rao Shastri, <u>Women in the Sacred Laws</u> (Bombay: Bharatiya Vidya Bhavan, 1959), p. 19.

26. <u>The Hindu Family,</u> pp. 201-202.

27. Aileen D. Ross, related in private conversation.

Chapter V

WORK: AN EMERGING VALUE
FOR DAUGHTERS OF THE MIDDLE CLASS

Whether their daughters should be allowed to work is a new decision for middle class Indian families. How they make this decision is the subject of this chapter. Examination of the current employment status of the respondents provides another perspective: how the question is answered in behavior as well as by verbalized attitude. The educated woman who is permitted to work is faced with the related problem of finding suitable employment, which is dealt with in the following chapter. Her less-educated sisters may be barred from employment simply because there are no "respectable" positions available to such middle class women.

In her first Bangalore study, Ross observed an increase in the numbers of urban middle class women who were entering paid employment. However, this change is so recent that studies made since Independence still stress the relative absence of this group in the labor force. Many attitudinal surveys show that there are still strong sentiments and social pressures against female employment. Little empirical research has involved educated women themselves. [1]

The Mysore Population Study, a carefully done sample survey jointly sponsored by the United Nations and the Government of India, provides factual data about the limited employment of middle-class women in Bangalore, as follows:

> A large share of the Bangalore labour force is engaged in personal services and related occupations, amounting to 13 per cent of the males and 33 per cent of the females. This situation is indicative of an insufficient opportunity for employment in more remunerative and more attractive jobs.... The concentration of the female labour force in such occupations, together with the small numbers of women in clerical, sales, and similar jobs, im-

plies that on the whole the employment of women
of higher social and economic status is not customary in Bangalore to nearly so great an extent
as in the cities of economically more advanced
countries.   Apparently those women who work in
Bangalore come chiefly from low-income families,
and they are presumably compelled to work by
economic necessity. [2]

That social attitudes strongly opposed the idea of
women working is pointed out by Goode, quoting various
polls:

> Public opinion is ... clearly against the idea of
> women working.   In the November 1955 Public
> Opinion Survey, 24 per cent of the respondents
> were in favor of a married daughter taking a job;
> but only 15 per cent of mothers in the sample ap-
> proved it.   Even among the sample's young and
> better-educated strata, only 28 per cent were in
> favor ....   In October of the same year, 70 per
> cent of the Delhi sample said they would not allow
> a young unmarried daughter or sister to go out
> and work.   As in most other areas of family opin-
> ion, the West Bengali and Calcutta respondents are
> more liberal: 46.5 per cent of the rural and 49
> per cent of the urban West Bengali were opposed,
> and only 33 per cent of the Calcutta respondents
> were so opposed.   Although the differences are
> great, widespread opposition is evident. [3]

Although South India is generally considered more conservative than some of the other cities mentioned, Ross found that
two-thirds of the 62 men in her Bangalore sample were in
favor of women "having a career. "[4] Her study contains
more recent opinion information than most of those cited
by Goode.   However, Goode has suggested that because
Ross' question was asked in a general way, rather than
referring to female members of the respondent's own family, a greater number of positive answers may have been obtained.   Ross found the women in her sample to be more
conservative than men, pointing out that:

> ... less than a third of the seventy-one women re-
> plying were favourable to the idea (of careers for
> women) although about 50 per cent more thought
> women should have careers in certain circum-
> stances. [5]

In her later study of female college students, the
same author found that "only a small proportion of the students were themselves seriously interested in careers. "[6]
While two-thirds of the 91 women included said that they
wanted to study for higher degrees, Ross dismisses these
answers as being given without serious thought.   Regarding
their future employment, she adds, "It is one thing for a
student to say that she would like to work after she graduates, and quite another matter for her to do so. "[7]

In spite of this, Ross, along with others, suggests
that economic reasons push the educated woman into work.
At the time of her first study, the economic pressures in
Mysore State were not considered as severe as those in
some other parts of India.   In quoting the 1951 Census of
Mysore State on this question, she suggests that economic
problems may provide the impetus for women to enter the
labor market:

> The actual number of women holding remunerative
> jobs is low in Mysore State compared with the rest
> of India.   The Census of Mysore states that the
> main reason for this is that the pressure for a
> higher standard of living has not yet been felt in
> the state to the extent it has in provinces contain-
> ing more and larger cities.   In large cities many
> of the middle-and-upper class families will have
> to live in small, expensive apartments.   This will
> give the women more leisure time for jobs outside
> the home and will also put more pressure on them
> to add to the family income.   Indeed, the main
> reason that so many married Hindu middle-class
> women work without reproach is because everyone
> understands the economic problems of the middle
> class, and that a wife's income is often essential
> to the family's standard of living. [8]

Goode, in his excellent theoretical analysis, repeated-
ly points to the structure of opportunities, as well as attitudes, as factors affecting women's employment.   Thus, for
example, he shows that the percentage of female workers in
factories fell between 1950 and 1956, during a period of
male under-employment.   And writing of India in 1963, he
could maintain:

> ... the opposition to a woman entering paid work is
> great, but at present her opportunities are few and

ill-paid. The cost in social standing is not ade-
quately compensated for by the small income, or
the greater richness of her life. Moreover, sinc
marriage still occurs at a relatively young age, i
the educated girl attempts to establish a genuine
career, she may miss her only chance at marriage.

Our data suggest that both opportunities and sentimer
have changed. Given current conditions, the movement of
the educated woman into the world of work becomes an obvious transition from college or post-graduate studies. Re
garding increased opportunities, Ross notes:

> The trend toward women working outside the hom
> in India has been accelerated by the new job oppo
> tunities opened up by industrialization, particular
> in the white-collar categories of employment. Th
> Five Year Plans of the Indian government have
> also publicized the growing need for trained and
> professional workers in many fields, and this cer
> tainty of work has probably encouraged many won
> en to train for these occupations. [10]

As will be seen, parental attitudes of the majority c
women are permissive of, or favor, their employment. In
order to understand this apparent modification in sentiment
one must look at other cultural values as well as notions
about women.

It has been indicated that middle class Indian famili
are beginning to value the education of their daughters as
well as their sons and that the woman graduate may be
sought as a bride by highly educated men. Thus, the initi
bachelor's degree has value for the graduate both as a wor
an and as a family member. But obtaining one's first degree sets off a chain of consequences which often leads to
taking graduate studies or obtaining a job.

The young woman's education qualifies her for respectable positions which are difficult for the family to oppose. [11] There is a strong feeling that "education should
not be wasted." Furthermore, jobs have become available
at a time when many Bangalore families feel affected by th
economic pressures known to characterize middle class fa
lies in other cities. To maintain a desirable standard of
living, provide the best possible education for all of one's
children, and meet the dowry demands of highly educated

bridegrooms, creates tremendous financial burdens.

At the same time, the college experience has provided the young woman with greater freedom of movement than she has ever known before, and has accustomed her family to her daily absence from home. Having experienced the outside world, the educated woman is less likely to adjust happily to the confinement of the house. Parents who have trusted a daughter to go to college have difficulty in insisting that she remain at home after graduation. A minority of the parents of women in our sample are doing just this, because they view work as more worldly and threatening than the college campus. And we have noted that respondents themselves consider employment to be less beneficial than education to their marital chances.

The Indian government's expressed need for trained women to serve more traditionally-oriented ones in fields such as health, education, and welfare, helps to foster their employment. Thus, for example, the Education Commission Report of 1965 suggested that special provisions be made to entice woman teachers to villages. [12] During our year in Bangalore, the Family Planning office sought women with master's degrees in sociology for work in the city. If high salaries and prestigious ratings can be attached to these less customary jobs, it may be possible to attract the daughters of economically pressed and relatively liberal families. As will be seen, the number of fields entered by educated Bangalore women is small indeed.

As indicated in Chapter II, 44 per cent of respondents are employed, 30 per cent are studying for advanced degrees, and 24 per cent are neither working nor studying. Two per cent are doing unpaid religious work. Of the 51 women not presently working, seven had previously held jobs--making a total of 50, or more than half, who have had work experience. This proportion will rise as many of those studying for advanced degrees enter the labor force. Thus, in Bangalore, work has become an established pattern rather than an exception for the college-educated woman.

The experiences of respondents are dramatically different from those of their mothers both with regard to level of education attained and extensiveness of employment. It has already been stated that only eleven per cent of the mothers are working or have worked, and these constitute a more highly educated group than mothers who have not been employed.

TABLE 16: PERCENTAGE DISTRIBUTION OF RESPONDENTS BY RELIGION AND CASTE BY CURRENT EMPLOYMENT AND EDUCATIONAL ACTIVITY

Current Activity	% All Respondents	HINDU			NON-HINDU	
		% Total Hindu	% Brahman	% Other Hindu	% Moslem	% Christian
Studying	30	30	29	32	11[a]	40
Employed	44	45	45	45	44	40
Unemployed						
Seeking job	9	8	8	9	33	0
Not seeking job	14	16	18	14	11	7
Other[b]	2	0	0	0	0	13
(No.) 100%	(97)	(73)	(51)	(22)	(9)	(15)

Note: Percentages are rounded and thus do not total 100%.

a. Seven of the Moslem women have already obtained a second degree, which helps explain the small percentage now attending school.

b. One respondent is a member of a Catholic order. Another is the daughter of a Protestant minister who considers her unpaid religious and welfare work a "calling."

The experience of work for middle-class women is not confined to one religious group, or to groups other than Brahmins, as can be seen in Table 16. Only one of the nine Moslem women and one of the 15 Christian women are staying at home--that is, are neither studying, employed, nor seeking employment. [13] The fact that 45 per cent of the Brahmin women are working suggests that normative sanctions against work are diminishing, since this caste group has been very strict regarding the protection of its women.

Nine of those not employed nor in school are seeking employment. The remaining 14 in this group are being "kept busy" at home. They are probably well-represented by the statement of this 20-year-old, single Brahmin B. A. :

> I would like to work but my mother is dead against.... For us there is no need to work. In our family, none of the girls is in service. Mother thinks that it is below their dignity if they send their daughters to work.... We tried our best to convince our mother. When it did not work out, we are trying to find happiness in the house itself.

Comparing the income and class identification of the 14 at home with the rest of the sample one finds that they appear to come from a somewhat higher income level and class status, on the average. [14] Half of those staying at home had family incomes of 800 rupees a month or more, as contrasted with a third of the total. As will be seen later, family attitudes appear to significantly affect the decision to stay at home. Twelve of the 14 "stay-at-homes" have at least one important family member who does not want her to work. More than half of them are married, even though married women constitute only 20 per cent of the sample.

How is employment related to educational attainment? Acquisition of a second degree appears to signify intention to work. We suggested in Chapter III that parents who do not want their daughter to work may prevent her from studying past the first bachelor's degree. A married non-Brahmin Hindu explains why she is not allowed to study for a master's degree: "I like to study zoology M. Sc. , but my husband's people and husband will not allow, since I will not be allowed to work outside. Hence my education will be of no use. "[15]

Looking at Table 17, it can be seen that of the 28 women holding higher degrees, three-quarters are working and most of the others are either seeking work or studying for Ph. D's. One young woman is a nun and only one other is simply staying at home. This contrasts with 19 per cent of those holding only one degree who are at home.

TABLE 17: PERCENTAGE DISTRIBUTION OF RESPONDENTS
BY EDUCATIONAL LEVELS BY CURRENT EMPLOYMENT
AND EDUCATIONAL ACTIVITY

| | Highest Degree Held | |
Current Activity	B. A. ; B. Sc.	Higher*
Studying	39	7
Employed	32	75
Not employed		
Seeking work	9	11
Not seeking work	19	4
Doing unpaid religious work	1	4
Number	(69)	(28)

*Higher degrees include: Bachelor of Education and Bachelor of Law, for which a prior bachelor's degree is required; Master of Arts and Master of Science; and the M. B. B. S. , a medical degree.

The vast majority of respondents positively evaluate employment in preference to staying at home. Asked whether or not they would prefer to work if there were no financial need, 85 per cent respond affirmatively. Over 70 per cent of those at home and not seeking employment are willing to express dissatisfaction with their current status and state that they would prefer to work. If those seeking employment are included with this group, the percentage rises slightly. In proportion to their representation in the sample, the preference for work is about the same for married and single women.

While working has acquired sufficient legitimacy for "stay at homes" to verbalize a position contrary to that of family members, acting against the expressed wishes of the family has not. The number admitting to a preference for work probably represents a minimal figure, since the most dutiful women claim that their desires are guided by the wishes of their parents or husbands.

Fourteen women said they would prefer not to work if there were no financial need. Comparison of this group with the 14 who are actually at home is of interest. There is an overlap of four cases between them, representing those whose preference to stay at home coincides with their actual situation. Of those who would prefer not to work, five are employed, two are seeking work, three are studying, and four are actually at home. Those who are still studying have not had to confront the decision of whether or not to work, and possibly some may marry before it is imminent. But for 18 per cent of the respondents there is an expressed discrepancy between what they would like to do and what they are doing. Economic need as well as family attitudes appear to be operating in the situation.

The strong preference of respondents for work is unusual when contrasted with reported attitudes of women elsewhere in the world. In several western nations, a substantial proportion of both men and women prefer that women stay at home and not follow an occupation. The highest proportion of women saying they would like to work, even if they did not have to, occurred in a Detroit sample of women already in the labor force. Sixty-six per cent said they would work even if they did not have to, but more than half gave "noncareer" reasons--such as escape from the household. [16] However, these studies include other than college-educated women.

Goode hypothesizes that women are willing to seize new career opportunities where they have been in a socially and economically underprivileged position, and where men are unable to provide for them at an economic level viewed as adequate. He considers this to be a question of whether women have more to lose or to gain by working. Certainly from a short-run perspective, members of our sample do not perceive the disadvantages to be greater than the advantages. Work provides a continuation of the freedom of college days, and earning money a source of respect. Furthermore, the weighing of possible disadvantages to their future is left to parents, the persons most concerned with the problems of marital choice.

Others have suggested that it is misleading to esti-

mate a woman's interest in work in terms of "career."
Since studies show that many men are not career-oriented,
it should not surprise us to find that many women do not
see work from that perspective. As in the researches
quoted by Goode, members of our sample explain their
preference for work in terms other than its intrinsic value:
"to keep busy" was mentioned most often as a reason, receiving 37 per cent of the responses. A single Brahmin
studying for her master's degree explains what "keeping busy"
means to her: 'I would prefer to work because it would
mean that my time is usefully spent. It would keep me occupied and prevent me from falling into bad ways and having
bad ideas." Her reasoning suggests that this young woman
has accepted parental values about keeping busy: a traditional value is used to help justify a new behavior pattern.

Despite the efforts of their families to keep them
busy with correspondence courses, music lessons, needlework, or other arts, those at home frequently feel "bored."
The lack of activity because they are not free to travel
about, and the absence of telephones in all but the weal-
thiest of homes, breeds a sense of isolation. For those
who are married and away from their own family members,
this may be doubly so. For single women sitting at home
and waiting to be married, life becomes tedious.

"To make use of my education," receives 19 per cent
of the responses explaining desire to work. The comment
that education should not be wasted emerges in many contexts and, as a widely accepted value, may be used in argu-
ment by young women whose parents doubt the propriety of
work. "Should not be wasted" is a term which includes economic connotations, since particular degrees will have value
in the employment market.

However, a growing value among young women, the
desire for economic independence, is represented by 13 per
cent of the responses. Another 12 per cent express the desire to provide service to others. While an elite group of
women have demonstrated such interest through volunteer
activities in the past, the notion that one can contribute
through paid positions is relatively new. It suggests the
development of interests outside the family, and some al-
legiance to the broader society among some middle class
women. [17]

The enrichment of knowledge or experience is given

as another reason for working. Many women maintain that
work as well as college provides opportunities to meet different kinds of people and to widen their horizons. Only
6 per cent of the reasons indicate that work is desired because of interest in a particular field or enjoyment of work
itself.

Some respondents suggest that their own positive
evaluation of work is not shared by other graduates, and
that the dignity of work for women is still held in question.
A 22-year-old Brahmin B. Sc. added these comments at the
end of the interview:

> Further, I would like to add that most of the
> graduate women have a problem like whether to
> have their education be useful to others or not,
> and whether to mix with the uneducated persons,
> to help them as far as possible, to give them
> some knowledge about their society; and if they
> are poor, how to supplement their family income,
> etc. Some will feel that it is a great loss of dig-
> nity for them if they work, as some will think
> that only poor people will work.

And another Brahmin now studying for her Bachelor
of Education degree at an institution outside of Bangalore,
wrote as follows:

> The main problem of a lady graduate is what to do
> next. The jobs available are not suitable and so
> many idle away their time till a husband comes
> along.... Another problem is the fact that many
> educated girls scorn jobs because they feel they
> are too lowly in nature and acceptance of them
> will result in a loss of status. Girls should be
> taught the dignity of labour, which should be em-
> phasized in college. This will prevent the waste
> of so much talent and education.

These status considerations affect not only the decision to work but also the determination of whether or not
particular jobs are accepted.

The question discussed above offers respondents the
choice between working and staying at home. The general
question, "If you could do anything you wanted to in the next
two years, what would you do?" brought out an even stronger

preference for education.   Forty-one per cent of the sample
indicate that they would like to engage in further studies.
This includes both individuals studying for advanced degrees
as well as some of those who already have such degrees.
Unquestionably, graduate study is a highly desirable and
liberating activity for these young women, already in the
very upmost strata of their countrymen as far as education
is concerned.   College is a happy interlude that precedes
and postpones the taking on of responsibilities and adjustments.

TABLE 18:   PERCENTAGE DISTRIBUTION OF ACTIVITIES
DESIRED BY RESPONDENTS IN THE NEXT TWO YEARS

Activity	Per cent
Take up further studies	41
Get a job	18
Travel	9
Get married	7
Finish studies	6
Change job	5
Stay in same job	3
Miscellaneous	4
Don't know; no special desires	6
Number	(97)

Table 18 shows that almost one-fifth of the respondents hope to get a job in the next two years.   Other desired
activities include changing jobs or continuing in the same
one, foreign travel, finishing studies already begun and getting married.   Only 7 per cent choose marriage as their
immediate aspiration.   Many of these preferences appear to
be tied to the activity in which the respondent is now engaged.   Foreign travel need not be considered an extremely
remote possibility, since a number of educated Indians do
go abroad.   Two women in our sample had come to the
United States with their husbands.   Looking at the choices
by age, class, educational level, and income, we find no
particular patterning.

Caution should be exercised in interpreting these responses, which reflect cultural norms as well as personal

feelings.   The presupposition of freedom of choice is not
easy for respondents to make.   A strong feeling of fatalism
shows itself in such initial answers as, "That is in the hands
of God. "   As discussed in Chapter IV, reticence to display
interest in one's own potential marriage is culturally defined
for the Indian woman.   Marriage is probably under-represen-
ted as a goal, while the desire for education is secular and
acceptable enough to be stated openly.

And, of course, the Indian woman knows that her future course does not depend on her own preferences.   A
father characteristically "puts" his daughter into some academic field or "sends" his daughter into employment.   It
has already been suggested that the woman's role in determining her own future varies, and is partly dependent first, on
her willingness to express her views and then on the strength
of her persuasive powers in "convincing" parents of a particular viewpoint.

Before looking at the reported attitudes of their family members about employment, a few facts about the economic role of these women should be considered.

If financial considerations are involved in their per-
mitting or advising a young woman to work, the family may
be expected to reap some benefits.   Our data suggests that
this is so, and that the economic duties of the sons of the
family are now shared by some of these educated daughters.[18]

Over three-quarters of the working respondents contribute more than half of their salaries to the family.   Besides the full-time workers, three women studying for advanced degrees are doing "tuitions" (tutoring).   Of the two
about whom we have information, one is giving her entire
earnings to the family while the other gives nothing.   However, in both cases, they are assisting their families financially.   The individual who keeps her earnings pays for all
of her own expenses, including clothing and gifts.

The pattern of handling salaries is also of interest.
Three patterns are found: the most traditional, in which the
whole salary is given to the head of the family and money
requested as needed; an intermediate one in which the salary
is turned in but a specific allowance returned; and the most
innovative, in which the employed woman keeps her whole
salary and handles many of her own expenses.   The intermediate pattern appears to predominate.   Ten women receive

money as needed; 29 receive specified allowances, and only
four keep their salaries.   The most frequent amount of allowance is between 21 and 50 rupees monthly.

Cormack reports on dissatisfaction among Indian students with the procedure of having to request money rather
than receiving a set allowance. [19]   Future studies of working
women might include consideration of these patterns and
their possible correlation with changing styles of family life.

While eight of the working respondents maintain that
it is their own idea to work, or that no one has influenced
them to do so, the other 35 name one or more relatives as
influential.   Members of the sample appear to have clearly
defined notions about how various members of the family
feel about their working.   It is obviously a topic which has
been discussed in the family.

The father, alone and in combination with other family members, is mentioned by 37 per cent of the respondents
as the relative who has had most influence about his daughter's employment.   Mothers, brothers, and sisters follow in
that order.   However, from answers to another question, it
is clear that had we asked the women staying at home, who
had influenced them not to work, husbands and parents-in-
law would have found significant representation.

The continuing influence of the father in the life of
his unmarried daughters was demonstrated in many ways
during the interviews.   Regardless of how many family members enter into decision-making within the family, the father's
formal role is clear.   He carries the main responsibility and
duty of protecting his daughters and assuring their future. [20]
If there is a question about the young woman's education, and
inquiries must be made, he is the appropriate person who
visits the authorities.   In contacts with the world outside the
family, he acts for them.   This does not mean that the father always plays the dominant role in all decision-making.
However, in both the areas of education and work he is far
more likely to be knowledgeable than his usually less well-
educated and more isolated spouse.   One well-educated father we knew told us that he hoped to put his daughter into
post-graduate studies but expected a period of opposition
from his wife.

Each respondent was asked how the following members of her family felt about her working: father, mother,

eldest brother (brother 1), next eldest brother (brother 2),
third eldest brother (brother 3), sisters as a group, husband
or fiancé where relevant, and "other" relatives who affect
decision making within her family.   If the respondent was
not employed, she was asked how family members would
feel about her seeking employment.   Most women answered
readily, differentiating between the views of significant family members, such as two or three elder brothers. [21]   A five
point scale of statements was given, ranging from "strongly
encourages" her to work to "prefers me to stay at home, "
with the middle category suggesting neutrality or permissiveness.   In some of the discussion that follows, the first two
and last two statements, respectively, are combined, making
a three point scale.

As other influential relatives, ten respondents name
parents-in-law, while 29 name such relatives as uncles,
aunts, grandparents and brothers-in-law.   Among this group,
uncles are mentioned most frequently.   In the majority of
cases, the immediate family, parents-in-law, and the respondent herself are most involved in decision-making about
work.

Now let us look at the most significant reference figures for our respondents (Table 19).   The largest number
of each type of family member encourages the young woman
to work, rather than taking a neutral position or preferring
that she remain at home.   It is of interest that in-laws are
said to hold a more negative viewpoint than members of the
family of orientation.   Half of the in-laws whose opinions
are known prefer that the daughter-in-law stay at home.
Such opinions need not be associated with the in-law role,
but may reflect a greater conservatism on the part of the
husband's family.   For example, the parents-in-law may not
permit their own daughters to work.   On the other hand,
keeping her at home may be considered a necessary way of
socializing the daughter-in-law into her new family role.

The strongest encouragement comes from the woman's
sisters, with 69 per cent of them favoring her employment.
Almost none are reported as preferring that she remain at
home.   Their sisters' concurrence demonstrates that the ap-
peal of work is shared by many young women besides those
in our sample.   More than two-fifths of the fathers and
mothers also encourage the respondents to work.   The last
is a surprising figure, considering the conservatism generally
attributed to Indian mothers.   It is rather unlikely that

TABLE 19: REPORTED ATTITUDES OF FAMILY MEMBERS ABOUT RESPONDENT'S WORKING

Family Members Reported Attitude	Father		Mother		Brother 1		Brother 2		Brother 3		Sisters		Husband[a]		In-Laws	
	No.	%	No.	%	No.	%	No.	%	No.	%	No.	%	No.	%	No.	%
Total[b]	77	100	86	100	57	100	36	100	18	100	65	100	20	100	10	100
Encourages her to work	33	43	39	45	31	54	17	47	7	39	45	69	10	50	3	30
Neutral	30	39	29	34	20	35	14	39	6	33	17	26	5	25	2	20
Prefers her to stay at home	11	14	16	19	5	9	5	14	5	28	1	2	5	25	5	50
Other[c]	3	4	2	2	1	2	0	0	0	0	2	3	0	0	0	0

a. One future husband of an engaged woman is included.

b. Totals represent living family members who are considered as having influence by the respondent. Eight married women gave no information on in-laws.

c. Other represents opinions which could not be classified according to the scale.

mothers would encourage behavior considered detrimental to their daughters' futures. A plausible conclusion is not that mothers are becoming less conservative or less interested in their daughters, but that proscriptions against work have become much weaker. Nor are mothers simply agreeing with their husbands, as will be seen when we turn to family agreement and disagreement. More than half of the eldest brothers but less than ten per cent of the third eldest brothers want the respondent to work. The latter group also tend to be less neutral than other relatives, and we find more than one-quarter of them preferring their sister to stay at home. More would have to be known about the effect of size of family and relationships of brothers and sisters in order to interpret this rather interesting finding. [22]

Fifty per cent of the husbands encourage their wives to work, while a quarter want them to remain at home. All family opinions refer to the respondent in her current marital status, yet the percentage of husbands wanting their wives to remain at home is larger than that of any of her other relatives, except the third brother and the husband's own parents. The husbands' attitudes are more conservative than those of their wives' fathers, but are unusually permissive when compared to those of Indian males questioned in previous surveys. [23]

The fact that so many husbands encourage their wives to work suggests the beginning of a pattern in which educated wives may be expected to help out financially in the early stages of marriage, much as they do in other societies. Whether or not a working wife will play her traditionally subservient role is a question that has been raised in other contexts. Some doubt may be raised also, about her willingness to go back to the confines of home after a period of work, and about the family's ability to withstand loss of her earnings. The hypothesis is suggested that many of these educated women will continue to work throughout the course of their married years.

It is now possible to compare the estimated opinions of relatives of women "at home" with the rest of the sample. A significantly higher proportion of fathers, mothers and husbands of those at home prefer that women not work, as seen in Table 20.

Mothers again prove to be less neutral than fathers, with fewer taking the middle, or permissive, position. More

TABLE 20: CURRENT STATUS OF RESPONDENTS BY ATTITUDES OF SELECTED FAMILY MEMBERS

Family Attitudes	Working or Seeking Work		Studying		At Home	
	No.	%	No.	%	No.	%
Father						
Encourages work	24	59	8	40	1	8
Is Neutral	14	34	11	55	5	42
Prefers her Home	3	7	1	5	6	50
Total[a]	41	100	20	100	12	100
Mother						
Encourages work	24	51	13	57	2	14
Is Neutral	17	36	8	35	4	29
Prefers her Home	6	13	2	9	8	57
Total	47	100	23	101	14	100

Brother 1						
Encourages work	17	61	9	47	4	50
Neutral	10	36	8	42	2	25
Prefers her Home	1	4	2	11	2	25
Total	28	101	19	100	8	100
Husband[b]						
Encourages work	9	90	1	100	0	0
Neutral	1	10	0	0	4	44
Prefers her Home	0	0	0	0	5	56
Total	10	100	1	100	9	100

a. N = 95. Totals represent living family members who are considered as having influence by the respondent. Opinions which could not be classified according to the scale are omitted. Percentages vary slightly from Table 19, in which N = 97.

b. One future husband of an engaged woman is included.

than half prefer the daughter to stay at home, and only two
of the 14 actually encourage her to work.   Eight of the wom-
en at home are married and one is to be married soon;
none of the husbands or future husbands encourage them to
work.   However, some are rated as neutral by their wives.

As mentioned earlier in the chapter, when the relatives' opinions of each of the 14 "stay at homes" are examined, we find that 12 have at least one important relative
who prefers that she stay at home. [24]   In contrast, only four
of the 43 employed women have any important relative who
takes that position. [25]   These findings demonstrate that, for
the most part, educated women in Bangalore do not go to
work or "take up jobs" as it is termed, without the agreement of their parents or husbands, if married.

We noted that there are 14 women who say they
would prefer not to work if there were no financial need.
Relatives of this group of 14 are not as strongly against
work as are those of the 14 who do not work.   Less than
half of the first group have at least one important relative
who prefers that she stay at home.   The desire to remain
at home, then, need not be a reflection of family views.   On
the other hand, some parents may have reluctantly permitted
their daughters to work due to economic circumstances, without considering it desirable.   Or they might insist that the
woman work if her earnings are needed.

Those women who are studying for advanced degrees
tend to report that their families' views are permissive more
often than do others.   Although such families have not yet
had to face the immediate prospect of the daughter's employment, they are not likely to oppose it.   This is borne out
in Table 20, above, in which very low percentages of families having daughters in advanced studies take the position
that they would prefer her to remain at home.

It is interesting to note the degree of family consensus about whether or not a daughter should work.   Since
opinions on the matter appear to be changing, we may expect
some disagreement among members of the same family.
Agreement and disagreement within a family can be assessed
by pairing each family member with the others. [26]   Disagreement is rated mild if two members hold adjacent viewpoints
on the five-point scale described on page 111.   It is rated
strong if their views are more than two intervals apart.
Averaging the paired agreements and disagreements of all

family members, the average rate of agreement is 59 per cent, of mild disagreement only 5 per cent, and of strong disagreement 26 per cent. Degree of agreement could not be judged in an average of 4 per cent of the pairings.

Only 38 families are found in which all members whose views are known are in agreement. Looking at the status of respondents in these families, 20 are working, 11 are studying, five are seeking work, and two are at home. Apparently family consensus is not required for a daughter to remain at home, but is necessary in order to support the departure from custom represented by employment. All but three of the families which are unanimous in their views either encourage or are permissive of the woman's working. The neutral or permissive position on the part of her family is evidently all that is needed to enable a young woman to work.

Only two cases occur in which the family prefers a daughter to remain at home but is allowing her to work or to seek work. Economic necessity may be the reason for their behavior. It is also likely that once it has become necessary for a woman to work, the family will find reasons to support and justify her doing so.

Family size and composition will undoubtedly affect the degree of agreement and disagreement found among its members. A more detailed analysis of family opinions would have to consider such questions as the relative authority of various members, the birth position of siblings, and the presence or absence of fathers or brothers. The possibilities for disagreement are, of course, greater if more family members are entering into discussion. On the average, a smaller number of family members' opinions were presented for comparison in those families where there was agreement on the issue of women's employment than was true of all families. However, if the views of the second and third brothers are excluded from all family comparisons, the total number of families which are in agreement does not change.

The paired comparisons of family members do not reveal dramatic alignments based solely on age or sex. The second eldest brother varies from the eldest in his alignment of views. The presence of a second eldest brother (as occurred in more than a third of the cases) may be important in families in which there is already dissensus.

While brother one and brother three are more often in agree
ment with the father than with their sisters, brother two
shows greater agreement with the sisters.   On the subject
under discussion, he shares the views of his father less
often than those of any other family member, a pattern in
which he resembles sisters rather than brothers.   However,
a proportionately higher percentage of brother two's differen
ces with other family members are described as mild rather
than strong in nature.

        Almost half of the sisters disagree with either their
fathers or mothers, or both.   This evidence of independent
thinking might not be readily observable, since their views
are being reported by the respondents, their sisters.   In
fact, these views may or may not be stated openly to elders
At any rate, since sisters are low in authority, their support of a woman who wants to work probably does not weigh
heavily.   It might be noted that one-third of the mothers
disagree, either mildly or strongly, with the fathers.   However, this does not mean that any of the disagreement will
be made known outside of the family circle.

        In countries where single women are free to work be
fore marriage, such as in the United States, there has been
continuing opposition to the employment of mothers.   It is
only in recent decades that mothers of young children have
entered the labor force in large numbers.   And even today,
only two-fifths of the married women in the United States
hold jobs. [27]

        India's case is different.   For centuries many pro-
scriptions were built around the need to protect the chastity
and honor of the unmarried female.   Employment was viewed
as a hazard which exposed her to too many temptations and
hence could sully her value and prevent the attainment of
her most important future role, that of wife.

        In the last chapter (Table 13) it was observed that
fewer than 40 per cent of respondents consider employment
an asset in finding a suitable mate.   Another 38 per cent
view employment as neither positive nor negative, and only
about one-quarter of them feel it is harmful to marital
chances.   The hypothesis that norms against the employment
of single females have weakened among this urban group is
supported by our data.

        It was also noted (Table 14, Chapter IV) that the

most frequently mentioned explanation of the benefits of employment was that the bride could help her husband economically.   Those who believe that boys' families prefer employed girls mention the high cost of living and the fact that
families need several wage-earners.

On the other hand, respondents who still consider employment a hindrance in marital desirability mention the negative character traits attributed to employed women.   A Brahmin who is staying at home after receiving her B. A. states,
"It is a hindrance.   Our community feels it is a hindrance.
Boys' parents think the girl is not domestic and doesn't
know anything about the house. "   And a married woman
agrees with this point of view, saying, "It hinders.   Indians
are not so broad-minded to accept employed girls.   They
will have some bad opinion.   They think the girls are care-
less and character-less. "   A related opinion is given by a
Christian, who holds a law degree, as follows:

> It depends--there are still certain families who
> like to think that the incoming daughter has not
> ventured beyond the four walls, except to a girl's
> institution and back.   Teaching would be least ob-
> jectionable.

Thus, a number of women feel that an employed female might still be expected to evidence such negative traits
as questionable moral character, lack of domesticity, or
too much independence.   The surprising fact is that so few
share these views.

The small group of 19 married women in the sample
will be examined to see if marital status is a determining
factor in whether or not an educated woman works.   Somewhat fewer than one-third of the married women, compared
to 49 per cent of the single ones, are working.   The young
wife who is seeking employment may be presumed to have
the support of her husband, since she would be unlikely to
go against his wishes.   If we include the women who are
seeking employment as well as those now employed, the picture changes.   Ten of the married women (53 per cent) and
42 (55 per cent) of the single women may be considered
available for the labor force.

The fact that work is not proscribed for married wom-
en may seem less surprising if one recognizes that divorce
is almost nonexistent in India, that duty toward one's husband

is a prime value, and that the married woman, being sexual satisfied, is presumed to be less vulnerable. Thus she may safely be given more freedom than her single sisters. What of the young mother?

On the question of whether or not the birth of a child puts an end to participation in the labor force, the experience of the seven mothers in the sample can be considered. Of the seven, four are working, and one is trying hard to obtain work. An additional young mother has just been delivered of her first child and is not in a position to work. On the other hand, of the 12 married but childless women, half are neither working, seeking work, nor studying. Thus a higher proportion of mothers than of childless wives are working or seeking work. While these facts could be discounted because of the small sample, they seem meaningful.

Financial reasons may well be involved in the employment of these mothers. As we will see below, respondents strongly support the participation of mothers in the labor force when economically necessary. In addition, the Indian wife who has borne a child acquires more prestige within her new family, and may be given greater freedom. Although in-law families are anxious to observe the young bride in her apprenticeship days, they may loosen the reins once she has proven herself by having a child. As can be seen in Table 21, respondents, who undoubtedly recognize the pressures on new brides, strongly favor the right of the childless woman to work, and thereby to escape the possible opprobrium of anxious parents-in-law.

Asked to define the conditions under which they think that a married woman who has no children should work, only two individuals categorically state that married women should not work.

Table 21 shows that a different major reason serves to justify the employment of childless wives as compared to mothers. "To keep herself occupied" is mentioned most frequently for the childless wives and least frequently for mothers. Financial reasons are overwhelmingly stressed in explaining why a mother may work, and they are second in importance for childless wives. These answers suggest that views about women's employment are closely related to, rather than in conflict with, their family roles. The cultural implication of childlessness is that it is a condition to be pitied. Many answers reveal the belief that a childless

TABLE 21: RESPONDENTS' VIEWS OF CONDITIONS
UNDER WHICH MARRIED WOMAN OR MOTHER MAY WORK

Condition	Married, no children		Mother	
	No.	%	No.	%
Keep self occupied	61	44	2	2
If financial difficulties arise	39	28	77	66
If she likes	10	7	4	3
Make use of education; do something useful	10	7	3	3
If husband allows	10	7	--	--
If someone looks after household and children	--	--	15	13
If children are grown	--	--	9	8
Other	9	7	6	5
Total	139	100	116	100

woman is subject to brooding and unhappiness if she is not
kept busy. A childless marriage does not constitute a ful-
filled family role for the wife, and she is expected to need
outside interests to compensate for the loss. In phrasing
this question the Western practice, where wives frequently
postpone motherhood in order to work for a short while, was
an obvious influence. However, the phrase, "a married woman without children," has a different meaning in India. Here
are some typical comments, the first by a 22-year-old non-
Brahmin Hindu, who says, "If the family worries her too
much about her not getting children, and she takes it to
heart, it is better to work, to keep her mind engaged. If
not, and she be quite rich, she may do some social services."

A Brahmin M.A. voices similar sentiments: "If she
feels frustrated and sad and that she is wasting her time
without doing any useful work, I feel she should work outside
the home. "

And a Moslem M. A. expresses the same point of view "It is better for her to work outside the home. Thus, she would be engaged and it will lessen the idea of the loss."

The vast majority of the sample believes that mothers should work if there is economic need. As is true of most societies, a mother's role is supposed to include emotional support and personal care of her children--except if the individual is compelled to sacrifice these emotional components for more pressing economic needs. Widowhood, absence of male economic support, and destitution have always been a part of life in India; it is far from uncommon for women to support their children. Today, the cost of living and desire for decent standards by the middle class help to include women from this class in the ranks of the employed. Viewed in this light, work is a support for, rather than a threat to, the family.

Representatives of the three religious groups in our sample express their reasoning on the matter as follows.

A 23-year-old non-Brahmin Hindu doctor states simply, "A mother can work outside whenever their material resources are not enough to lead a better life."

A 21-year-old Christian justifies employment this way: "To meet the financial problems [she can work]. To give better comforts to her children."

And a Moslem M. A. says, "Only if she has no other source to bring up her children, or if the husband's income is less, to keep up the standard of living."

Other conditions mentioned receive many fewer responses. One-fifth of the answers include the provision that the mother's working should not adversely affect her children. A tiny 4 per cent of those interviewed categorically state that a mother should not work. However, an equally small percentage of responses permissive of employment would allow a mother to work "if she likes" or "to keep self occupied," reasons which suggest personal interests. Such reasons might be added after a set of more compelling ones, as in this answer given by a working mother of two:

> First, if separated or widowed. Second, financial. If she's interested, it's all right too, just for interest--even if she's rich. My mother takes care

of my children, so it's not as if a servant were there.

A Brahmin Ph. D. candidate was one of the few who mentions use of the mother's talents for society at large rather than just for the family's benefit:

First consideration is financial. Second is if the mother is a woman of talents and intellect, her usefulness should not be confined only to her home. It could be utilized to improve our nation in any manner.

It should be noted that this viewpoint is very rare and is not fully accepted even in highly industrialized societies such as the United States.

As a final note to this chapter, it should be added that viewpoints about work seem unrelated to the caste or religious background of members of the sample. Rosen's assertion that class divisions begin to assume more importance than caste in the city is supported by much of this data, for the group under study.

Now that urban middle class women are increasingly permitted to work, their problems in finding suitable employment and the jobs they actually hold should be examined.

Notes

1. Amarjit Mahajan reports on a study of the intentions to work of female students at Punjab University, Chandigarh. Of his sample of 237 college students, 215 or 91 per cent said they would like to take up employment. "Women's Two Roles: A Study of Role Conflict, " Indian Journal of Social Work 26, no. 4 (January 1966): 378.

2. The Mysore Population Study: A Cooperative Project of the United Nations and the Government of India (New York: Dept. of Economics and Social Affairs, United Nations, 1961). Field work was carried out between December 1951 and September 1952.

3. William J. Goode, World Revolution and Family Patterns (London: Collier-Macmillan, 1963), p. 269.

4. Aileen D. Ross, The Hindu Family in Its Urban Setting
    (Toronto: University of Toronto Press, 1961), p.
    201.

5. Ibid.   Ross did not claim scientific validity for her
    sample, which was composed of middle and upper
    class persons selected by her Indian interviewers.
    The sampling validity of some other Indian studies
    quoted by Goode may also be questioned, as he
    makes clear.   However, they are all that is availa-
    ble.

6. Student Unrest in India (Montreal: McGill-Queen's
    University Press, 1969), p.   181.

7. Ibid. , p.   187.

8. The Hindu Family, p.   198.

9. Goode, op. cit. , p.   269.

10. Student Unrest, p.   187.

11. Respondents spoke of sisters or sisters-in-law who
    were not college graduates and who were not em-
    ployed.   A study of the employment rates of less
    well-educated middle class women would be instruc-
    tive.

12. Report of the Education Commission, Education and
    National Development [The "Kothari Report"] (New
    Delhi: Government of India Press, 1966), p.   64.

13. Seeking employment need not be a very active process.
    It often consists of submitting one's name to the
    Government Employment Exchange and waiting to
    be called.   A period of waiting for results usually
    follows a job interview or examination.

14. However, dichotomizing income and class of the "stay at
    homes" and all others, the relationship is not sta-
    tistically significant in either case.

15. The interviewer was assured that, even though she is
    not allowed to study further, the respondent feels
    "quite happy, " since she is obeying her husband and
    her in-laws.   "This she feels is her most important
    duty, " commented the interviewer.

16. Goode, op. cit., pp. 63-64.

17. In response to another question about whether or not an educated woman should be expected to contribute to society in any special ways, a number of idealistic responses mentioned duty to "my India" or "my less fortunate sisters."

18. Ross, The Hindu Family, notes the development of this pattern. At first educated women volunteer to aid the family; later they may be expected to do so.

19. Margaret L. Cormack, She Who Rides a Peacock, (Bombay: Asia Publishing House, 1961), p. 52.

20. The loss of the father by death is seen as a serious blow to his daughter, who must now depend on less interested male relatives either to find a husband or take care of her for the rest of her life.

21. By significant is meant one who exercises the right to enter into family discussions on the topic. Respondents point out, for example, that the younger brothers "would have no opinions." Sisters' views, while often considered less important, are known and evidently enter into family discussions. Sometimes a sister was characterized as very "strong-willed"; one who presumably made her opinions known somewhat forcefully and held to them. In the few cases where various sisters were said to disagree, their opinion is marked "other."

22. The following is speculative: If a girl has three elder brothers, it is likely that the eldest not only is highest in authority but has a more distant relationship to her than does a brother nearer to her own age. One might expect the youngest brother to be more sympathetic to the woman's own wishes to work. The strange contrast between viewpoints of the eldest and third brother suggests a different interpretation. The brother who wants his sister to remain at home may feel he is being protective. The brother who encourages her to work may be thinking of her economic contribution rather than her own wishes. Dichotomizing brothers' viewpoints between those who prefer the respondent to stay at home, and those who are encouraging or permissive, we find a sta-

tistically significant difference between the opinions of brothers one, two and three.   Chi-square = 6. 376 d. f. = 2, and the relationship is significant at the . 05 level.

23.   See Goode, op. cit., p. 261.

24.   Here "important" includes mother, father, husband or in-laws.   Of the two remaining, one was a young married Brahmin who did not give the opinion of her in-laws.   She described herself as very wealthy and as being interested in doing volunteer work.   The other was a single Moslem M. A. whose family would have permitted her to take a teaching position.   Willing to accept only college teaching herself, she had ceased looking for such posts after some refusals.

25.   This comparison between the employed women and the "stay-at-homes" yields a Chi-square of 29. 798, d. f. = 1.   The differences are significant at the . 001 level.   The only married respondent known to us who is going against the wishes of her parents and in-laws is a teaching assistant living in the United States with her husband and child.   She justifies working by saying that her in-laws and parents do not understand conditions in the United States.   Her husband approves of her employment.

26.   Brothers but not husbands are included in this analysis.

27.   Elizabeth Janeway, Man's World, Woman's Place, (New York: William Morrow, 1971), p. 26.

28.   He states: "In urban India caste is increasingly being replaced by individual and class relationships. . . . Class factors based on the role of an individual in the economy and society interact with caste elements. The caste and class factors both support and oppose each other, but class elements are more important than caste elements in understanding urban society and pressures. " [George Rosen, Democracy and Economic Change in India (Berkeley: University of California Press, 1966), pp. 33-34.]

Chapter VI

FINDING A SUITABLE JOB

Growing industrialization tends to increase opportunities for female workers even as it displaces many from
agriculture. Yet patterns of female employment vary among
countries which are at the same stage of industrialization.
Comparative research such as the following suggests that
tradition as well as economics influence labor patterns:

> It is difficult to account for these differences in
> occupational distribution (in different countries)
> by reference to the stage of economic development
> alone. An equally important factor in a great
> many cases seems to be the character and tradi-
> tions of the national economy.... Thus, in the
> great majority of countries studied, women form
> a high proportion (31 to 50 per cent) of all pro-
> fessional and technical workers; most women in
> this group are teachers and nurses, occupations
> traditionally recognized as women's jobs. Excep-
> tions are found in India and Pakistan, where wom-
> en form 17 per cent and 4 per cent respectively
> of all technical and professional workers. [1]

These observations find support here. While work,
in itself, no longer carries the same disreputable aura as
in the past, jobs defined as suitable for middle class Indian
women are still very limited. Indian traditions help explain
the lack of representation among the sample of the usually
typical occupations of nursing and social work. Medicine,
but never nursing, is referred to as an early aspiration by
some members of the sample. Social work is thought of as
volunteer service rather than as a paid occupation. The
school of social work in Bangalore had not yet been granted
formal government accreditation at the time of the study. [2]
Until that occurs, its graduates receive a diploma which is
not worth as much as a degree. This lack of status reflects
the lack of recognition accorded paid social work in Ban-

galore. [3]   But while traditional attitudes toward social work
have hampered its development as a professional field, there
are indications that the situation may change.   Among these
are the following: the presence of highly regarded schools
of social work as models in a few major Indian cities, the
high educational and professional qualifications of the present
director of the Bangalore school, and the importance of
trained social workers in promoting the national goal of
family planning. [4]

It should be mentioned that social work, as an avocation, has provided an outlet for the talents of a small group
of educated elite women, some of whom wield real power.
They perform the work of executives without pay, and may
actively seek social reforms.   It is from this class of wom-
en that most of the female political leaders of India have
come.

Library science is a newly developing field which
may provide another occupational choice but which has not
as yet achieved recognition in Bangalore.   The one respondent studying library science will receive a technical diploma
rather than the more valuable advanced degree.   However,
the undisputed respectability of library work presages its
potential popularity.

Jobs are thought of in terms of "suitability," which
includes consideration not only of the special limitations imposed on middle class females but also more general norms
defining appropriate work for the educated.   We shall see
that many of the concerns of respondents relate to their position as educated persons as well as to their status as
women.   Potentials for change--movement into new types
of work--grow out of the first area of concern.   Thus, if
high prestige and remuneration can be accorded to positions
in family planning, for example, part of the objection to
this work can be mitigated.   At the time of the study, persons with master's degrees were being sought for family
planning jobs, and the high educational requirement alone
lent some prestige to a rather unacceptable field.

Of the 43 working respondents, 60 per cent are
teaching at various levels from lower school (primary
grades) through university, and 35 per cent hold clerical
or office jobs.   Two practicing physicians are also included
in the sample.

Clerical positions are mainly state or central government jobs in offices, factories, or in hospitals, and vary by grade and pay. The broadly used title "clerk," includes work of differing degrees of complexity. Clerical duties include such tasks as correspondence, writing of drafts or statistical reports, and messenger or library work within an office. One stenographer, one telephone operator, and two bank clerks are found in the sample.

The range of salaries paid to clerical workers, teachers, and physicians is shown in Table 22. [5] The median and modal income falls within 200 to 249 rupees per month.

While there is a fairly wide range of salaries among both clerical employees and teachers, their average salaries differ. The median income of all teachers, if we include college lecturers with others, is between 150 and 199 rupees per month, while the median income of those in clerical positions falls in the 200 to 249 rupees range. However, no college teacher earns less than 200 rupees. [6] The best paid clerical jobs are held by two women with bachelor of law degrees. Only two-fifths of the clerical workers earn as little as 199 rupees. The two physicians are obviously at the top of the income scale. At the bottom, eight teachers earn under 150 rupees and are the only workers earning so little.

Of the teachers of all types, 56 per cent hold a degree past the first bachelor's degree, whereas only one-third of the 15 clerical workers hold such degrees. Thus, while the average education of teachers is higher, their average salary is lower. However, matching up education with income, there is a significant correlation. Two-thirds of those holding only a B.A. or B. Sc. earn below 200 rupees per month, while three-quarters of those holding higher degrees earn above 200 rupees per month. The general belief that advanced education increases one's earning power is borne out by the facts, and is evidently true for both sexes.

The expression of general attitudes about work and the problems of educated working women tended to be offered more freely than answers about the respondent's own job. An individual respondent would more willingly point out that salaries are not commensurate with women's education than discuss the fact that her own salary was low. [7] This reti-

TABLE 22: RESPONDENTS' OCCUPATIONS BY SALARY

Rupees per month	Physician	Univ. Teacher	Teacher Below Univ.	Clerical	Total
Under 150	0	0	8	0	8
150-199	0	0	5	6	11
200-249	0	2	7	7	16
250-299	0	0	0	1	1
300-349	0	1	1	1	3
350-399	0	1	0	0	1
400 and over	2	0	0	0	2
Total	2	4	21	15	42*

*One respondent, working in the United States as a uni-
versity teaching assistant, was eliminated from this analysis because of differing wage scales. [Note: at the time
of the study, one rupee was worth about 13.5 cents in
American money at the official exchange rate.   A respondent earning the median income, between 200-249 rupees,
would be earning a maximum of about 33 American dollars
per month.   This equivalent is cited only as a matter of
interest, since costs and standards obviously differ widely
between the two countries.]

cence to talk negatively about one's own job can be explained
in several ways.   First, the overwhelmingly positive orientation to work rather than the alternative of sitting at home
may encourage women to suppress minor dissatisfactions.
Secondly, women have been taught that it is up to them to
adjust to what is required and demanded, rather than complain.   Third, there is the matter of pride and the belief
that one should not engage in activities below one's status
or educational qualifications.   A job deemed unsuitable may
be rejected even in cases of prolonged unemployment.   If it
is accepted, excuses may be made to save face.   Finally,
the formal interview situation probably inhibited some individuals from openly criticizing their jobs.   However, in informal conversations held with young women other than respondents, criticism also centered about conditions of employment and rates of pay rather than intrinsic aspects of
their work.

All of those interviewed were asked to describe the employment problems of educated women, if they believed that such exist. Twenty per cent maintain that it is not difficult for graduates to get work and envision no other problems. A few believe that there are some difficulties but cannot elaborate. Seventy-one describe one or more types of problems encountered by educated women, totalling 119 responses. These fall into several major categories: (1) the unavailability of appropriate jobs--26 per cent of responses; (2) the need for special types of qualifications, such as typing--25 per cent; (3) the use of criteria other than merit in determining appointments--20 per cent; (4) the general problem of unemployment--12 per cent; and (5) family and societal pressures on women who work--8 per cent. The remaining responses were vague or miscellaneous.

The highest percentage of responses concentrate in the area of the appropriateness of available jobs. Under this category are included statements about the inconvenience of hours or work places for women; the unsuitability of some work environments; the fact that salaries do not measure up to educational attainments; and the failure of available jobs to utilize one's education. Within this category, then, we find references to the problems of the educated in general and others which apply more specifically to women.

There is a strong implication in answers that it is demeaning to accept work which is beneath one's qualifications even if it be white collar work. In this hierarchical society, educated persons are familiar with the rank of job for which they qualify, especially since specific educational requirements are attached to government jobs. The large percentage of positions in the public sector, with clear-cut formal criteria of selection, enable the individual to assess the gap between jobs for which he is eligible and those which are available. One of the Indian interviewers, summarizing the views of a young Christian woman who holds a bachelor of law degree, writes:

> Her main problem was expressed with regard to her education and her job. She said that she hates to call herself a clerk after doing the Bachelor of Law. She expressed the view that after doing postgraduate study one would like to occupy a respectable position and not be called a clerk, which is looked down upon in society. With re-

spect to what she liked least about her job, she
said that though she took so much pains in draft-
ing letters, she couldn't subscribe her signature
on them.   Thus she felt her importance is not
felt. [8]

In the teaching field, too, jobs are ranked in terms
of prestige.   Since possession of a master's degree qualifies
one to be a college lecturer, some of those holding such degrees express the sentiment that teaching in a high school is
beneath them.   A Moslem M. A. , holding out for college
teaching or research as the only appropriate work, explains
her situation in this way:[9]

I want to do teaching or research.   I want only co
lege teaching.   Yes, I have tried at the government colleges.   I want to do a Ph. D. , but that,
too, is difficult.   Even though my family is educated, even to my grandfather, still our religion
influences things.   The girls can't go out freely.
Some of the jobs require working with many kinds
of people, like social work or family planning.
My family would allow only teaching or research.
That is what I prefer.

However, some women are beginning to question the
attitudes expressed above.   One who is studying for a bachelor's degree in education maintains that such feelings are due
to the lack of dignity accorded work.   She states:

Another problem is the fact that many educated
girls scorn jobs because they feel they are too
lowly in nature and acceptance of them will result
in a loss of status.   Girls should be taught the
dignity of labor, which should be emphasized in
colleges.   This will prevent the waste of so much
talent and education.

This concern with an appropriately prestigious job for
his daughter is expressed by a father as he suggests that
women are discriminated against:

There is still difficulty in getting suitable jobs.
She is teaching in a primary school near here,
but it is not very good.   It is only till she gets
a better job.   She put her name in the Employment Exchange over a year ago.   Only one offer

came in and it was not satisfactory. The Exchanges don't work so well. Many government offices are not hiring women. It is changing but it is still difficult.

Clerical work is rejected frequently because of the view that offices lack the "proper atmosphere" for women. A Brahmin teacher who resides with her brother and sister-in-law states, "My brothers don't like me to work in an office. I, too, like teaching. . . . Many girls are working in factories where the atmosphere is not nice." And a respondent who works as a clerk puts it this way: "If a girl gets a job, she must consider first whether it is a proper place. If there are rowdies there, she won't go. A boy can work anywhere, but in India a girl can't."

Another woman studying for her bachelor of education degree explained that she had been offered a job through the government employment exchange but "since it was clerical" she did not accept it.

The number of clerical workers is too small for detailed analysis, but it might be noted that none of the employed Moslem women are working in offices. Brahmins are also less well-represented than other cases in these castes in these posts.

Underlying assumptions about the special difficulties of members of their sex, as well as references to general employment problems are reflected in the interviews quoted above. Two women who hold master's degrees describe the problems of women very specifically, both stressing the issue of job location. The first, a Brahmin studying for her Ph. D. states:

I feel there is not much of a problem to get a job in Bangalore. But the suitability of environment or working conditions and the distances weigh much in a girl taking up employment. There are many jobs but the problem is one of transport and environment. There are many jobs in banks, but our Indian girls are rather shy, and they may not feel right if there are no other girls and many men. With some jobs, the hours are not so convenient. Work may end at 5:30, but with the buses she may not get home until eight. Most girls like to work in offices. The burden is not

too much, and it is shared. The government jobs
are more secure. But if they are lecturers in
government colleges, there is the problem of being
transferred.

And the other M. Sc. points out,

If they get a job, there is the question of whether
it is in Bangalore or out of Bangalore. Which
type of job she gets--it may be in her line or out
of her line. She may prefer to stay in Bangalore.
Even if the job is out of her line she may prefer
to work in Bangalore. She may take into consideration other facts--facilities, hostel or house in
a nice place, the type of living there. She has to
consider all these things.

Once again, the problem of finding respectable living
quarters away from home is articulated. This problem is
recognized in the Education Commission's proposal that more
attention be given to developing hostels for teachers. Parents who agree to allow their daughter to take an out-of-
town post may send along an elderly female relative as
chaperone.

Proximity to home is frequently a significant factor
in the family's decisions about a daughter's educational activities or place of work. The hypothesis might be tested
that permitted distance between home and work is an index
of the conservatism of the family. The relative prestige of
the position may prove to be a counter-balancing factor, however.

The inconvenience and delay of public transportation
in Bangalore is a proper excuse for any late arrival for appointments. In addition to the discomfort of long queues,
over-crowded and off-schedule buses, there is the matter of
returning home late in the evening. And of course the hours
kept by a single woman will be scrutinized by neighbors.
For those most orthodox, the girl's absence at work signifies
that she is away from parental supervision and perhaps in
the company of men. If, in addition, she returns home beyond the hour considered proper, her reputation may suffer.

The unmarried daughter is sometimes expected to eat
her meals at home, a difficult requirement if her job is any
distance away. Most middle class individuals observe the

custom of going home for lunch or of having hot meals brought to their place of work by a family servant or special functionary. [10]

The importance of eating meals prepared in one's own kitchen is great. There are caste prescriptions and taboos about who may handle food, and much distate for unfamiliar cooking. Family, religious, and caste styles of food preparation vary, and some Hindus do not like to eat food in cafeterias and restaurants. At the same time, hot meals are very much preferred. Most restaurants, except for a few expensive ones, are considered out of bounds to respectable women. They may be suspected of arranging a rendezvous with a man there. The expense of eating lunch out in a decent place is exorbitant. [11] A working woman's dilemma of where and how to have lunch is solved in several ways. Some parents restrict daughters to jobs near home, so that lunch can be taken in the usual fashion. Some Hindus eat a very early lunch before starting out for work, which frequently begins at 10 a. m. Offices may set working hours in such a manner as to include a long lunch period so that workers are able to travel home for their meal. Shops are frequently closed for two or three hours in mid-day.

The status of a job may determine the degree of time flexibility tolerated. Unmarried physicians are allowed to maintain unusual hours, since the prestige of the position is unquestioned. [12] Despite the greater permissiveness in this job category, place and conditions of work strongly influence the jobs that a respectable woman may take.

Turning now to some of the other categories of problems mentioned, a quarter of the responses deal with special qualifications that are needed. Certain degrees are considered better than others in the employment market; the B. Sc. , for example, is more valuable than the B. A. A bachelor of education degree (making one a "double graduate") entitles its possessor to better teaching posts in secondary schools. A master's degree qualifies one for the position of college lecturer or a higher clerical post. In some cases a degree is not sufficient in itself, and merit, in the form of graduating in the upper part of one's class is needed. A number of individuals spoke of a third class master's degree as being less valuable than a bachelor's degree. [13] However, "merit" was mentioned specifically as a special qualification only eight times. The role of influence was noted more frequently.

Among other special qualifications, almost a third of the responses indicate the value of technical skills such as typing or shorthand. Respondents spoke of taking up typing as a "side study" which would prove useful in obtaining employment. [14]

A fifth of the responses dealing with problems in work suggest that criteria other than merit are used in hiring applicants. The role of influence is mentioned far more often than any other criterion, such as sex, caste or religion. The term "influence" is used broadly and often includes within it the notion that considerations of caste or religion are significant. It sometimes serves as a ephemism for these terms, but may mean that family connections carry much weight. One respondent spoke proudly of obtaining a teaching post on her own even though her mother could readily have obtained one for her.

A Christian woman, working as an upper division clerk in a government factory was more explicitly critical of caste than most:

> India is not much progressed. Employment opportunities are few. Moreover, in the government offices itself they have this caste feeling and are very prejudiced. First thing they enquire about is caste. We can't talk about private concerns but the government itself does. It means there is no way for others to come up. Some people, though they don't possess any intelligence, will occupy high positions. Whereas brilliant students do not get, because of caste. I agree if they consider merit as the main criteria, but not caste.

And a wealthy Moslem woman, married to a physician, complains of religious prejudice:

> As far as my case is concerned, I think that being a minority--i.e., a Muslim--is a great setback in obtaining a job. Proof is that I, standing first in the University, could not get a job after applying in six colleges. That is why I'm very keen on going abroad and doing my Ph.D., and working abroad. [15]

Most respondents were less direct in mentioning caste influence, a topic which came up more frequently in informal contacts the author made. However, some respondents did complain that the official preference given to members of Scheduled Castes, through compensatory legislation, made things more difficult for members of other castes. As mentioned previously, only two members of the sample turn out to be from this "privileged" group. Those interviewed did not mention specifically another caste group which is highly influential in the city, and which is reputedly able to obtain preference for its own members in various appointments. This group, too, was not highly represented in the sample.

Discrimination on the basis of sex is barely mentioned. The following hypotheses may be offered: first, educated women presently compete with men in very few fields since they confine themselves to lower clerical posts and teaching. They are also considered essential in dealing with members of their own sex, so that, for example, female doctors have a natural clientele and are not considered unusual. The whole field of family planning is also one that requires not only trained workers but women, especially to serve members of their own sex. In order to recruit them, government becomes increasingly concerned with providing proper living quarters and incentives. Pressure is also exerted by the government employment exchanges, as they continue to offer family planning jobs to any qualified woman who places her name in the exchange. However, as women seek positions in fields more traditionally male, they may encounter more opposition. [16]

Secondly, the prevalence of other societal divisions seems to supercede that of sex, as in the case of the Moslem respondent quoted earlier. She interprets discrimination against her to be based on religion rather than sex or marital status. Women are now able to obtain a number of government jobs for which formal educational requirements are strongly emphasized. The same patterns of sexual discrimination in employment that one finds in a country such as the United States may not develop in India. The middle class women who take jobs based on their educational qualifications will be fitted into a stratified employment system based on those qualifications, aided or hindered by caste and family connections. Thus, sex may play a minor role in obtaining positions.

At present women are criticized for their shyness and unwillingness to enter untraditional fields, but should

they try to enter male domains, such as engineering, there
might be opposition. On the other hand, as has been mentioned, a small number of elite women have succeeded in
playing important roles in Indian history.   Such women may
enter politics, as they enter social work, as a duty to serve
others.   The advantages of coming from leading political
families, and having excellent educations, may enable some
women to operate as equals in the political sphere.   Within
the home, a woman has a prescribed relationship to her
father and husband--males of the same family position.   Out
side the home, the woman's class and caste position have
much to do with how she treats members of other classes
and castes, regardless of sex.

The role of sex in determining appropriate fields of
study may also work to the educated woman's advantage in
that the best male students are drawn off to medicine and
engineering.   This means that, for example, in a field such
as sociology, women students may predominate and may per
form better than their male co-students.   They are more
likely to do well on examinations and present good records
in seeking employment if they are competing with men who
were not able to obtain seats in more desirable fields.
Thirdly, the Central Government has been trying to equalize
the position of women and has opened up new educational and
employment opportunities.   Government enterprises, such as
arts and crafts emporia, employ many of them, some in
managerial positions.   A series of legal reforms has attempted to equalize the legal rights of women.   Remuneration for particular government posts is standardized, so that
women will receive the same rate of pay as men.

A little more than a tenth of the responses about
problems in work refer to the general problem of unemployment.   Concern about the large number of the "educated unemployed" young people in India has been voiced in many
quarters. [17]   As colleges open their doors to more students,
and as these graduate, the problem becomes more severe.
Respondents who express concern over unemployment usually
feel that opportunities should be improved for both men and
women.   One young woman who is studying for her master's
degree in economics has a different opinion, stating,

> It is hard for boys to get employment.   That's one
> of our big problems in India.   So I don't think
> girls should work unless there is financial diffi-
> culty.   For example, a girl took up a post here

and left after one year.   That took up a place a
boy could have had.   For us it is not so important,
as we won't be the main financial support, but for
a boy, he will work all his life, so it is important
for him.   That's what I think.   I don't know how
others feel [said somewhat defensively].   It is
easier for girls to get jobs.

Hers was definitely a minority viewpoint.

Ten persons specify that there are still family and
societal pressures against women working, such as the ones
already discussed.   At the same time, there are ways in
which these pressures are being counterbalanced.   The family which needs the daughter's salary to maintain its standard of living allows her to take a "suitable" job, or even
comes to view a respectably employed daughter-in-law as an
asset.   As work becomes more usual, it also becomes more
acceptable.   Then, when the more desirable types of jobs
are unavailable, women may be permitted to work in somewhat less satisfactory surroundings, as in the case of this
government factory clerk.   She comments, "Father didn't
want me to join the factory but there is no other job.   I
applied in X Bank, but didn't get, because a lot of recom-
mendation is needed there. "

As more middle class women enter the ranks of the
educated and subsequently the employed, further modifications
of norms will gradually take place.   A daughter who has
taught in a neighborhood school may be allowed to accept a
better position some distance away from home.   Parents
whose daughters have worked as teachers may permit one
of them to take a slightly less suitable job.

Such changes in parental attitudes are described by a
number of women.   As daughters acquire the qualifications
for prestigious positions, and the boldness to argue for
them, the titles and salary begin to outweigh past objections.
Thus, on the basis of what has already taken place we can
anticipate further gradual change--an increase in the kinds
of work in which middle class women may engage and less
restriction as to place of work.

Working respondents were given a range of choices
with which to describe their jobs in terms of convenience
or inconvenience (with regard to work, time and place) and
how interesting and tiring they are.   They were also asked

the extent to which they felt that their education had prepare
them for the job, what they specifically liked or disliked, an
what other job they might prefer.   Table 23 compares the
responses of different types of workers, and of those earning
higher and lower salaries, to some of these questions.

Even though the location of work place and hours of
work are important considerations in choice of jobs, they
are not always found to be satisfactory.   Forty-five per cent
of the respondents feel that either place or hours of work
are inconvenient.   There is a significant difference between
the convenience ratings of teachers and clerks, a finding
that is not surprising. [18]   The possibility of obtaining work
in a school that is near one's home is fairly good, since
schools are located in many different neighborhoods.   Govern
ment office buildings and factories are less likely to be near
the woman's residence.   A much higher proportion of teachers than clerks report that their work is very interesting,
the difference being statistically significant. [19]   Teachers
find their work more tiring than do clerks; more than half
of the latter consider their jobs "not at all tiring. "   This
suggests that they may sometimes find themselves with too
little to do.   A question on boredom would undoubtedly have
elicited more information on job satisfaction.

Over 80 per cent of the respondents feel that their
education was very much needed, or somewhat needed, for
their job, but the proportion is lower for clerks than for
teachers.   Even though clerks earn more, on the average,
than teachers, they evidence less job satisfaction.   There
is a significant relationship between jobs described as very
interesting and those for which one's education is considered
relevant. [20] Six of the eight women who maintain that their
education was hardly needed, or not needed at all, find their
jobs uninteresting.

When we divide the working sample into those who
earn above and below 200 rupees per month, we find fewer
distinctive contrasts.   Although a higher proportion of those
earning higher salaries appear to find their work interesting
the relationship is not statistically significant.

The question of whether or not a woman's education
is needed for her job was asked in a general way, and is
subject to varying interpretations.   A college degree may be
required for a particular job, and in the formal sense then,
the education is needed.   Whether or not one actually uses

TABLE 23: TYPE OF JOB AND SALARY EARNED BY RESPONDENT'S DESCRIPTION OF OWN JOB

Description of Own Job	Total		Physician		Teacher		Clerk		Salary Under Rs 200		Salary Over Rs 200	
	No.	%	No.	%	No.	%	No.	%	No.	%	No.	%
Total	42	100	2	100	25	100	15	100	19	100	23	100
Convenience of Time and Place of Work												
1. very convenient	22	52	0	0	18	72	4	27	10	53	13	57
2. somewhat or very inconvenient	19	45	2	100	6	24	11	73	8	42	10	43
3. not given	1	2	0	0	1	4	0	0	1	5	0	0
Whether Work is Tiring												
1. very or somewhat	28	67	2	100	19	76	7	47	11	58	15	65
2. not at all	14	33	0	0	6	24	8	53	8	42	8	35
Whether Work is Interesting												
1. very	25	60	2	100	19	76	4	27	10	53	16	70
2. somewhat or not at all	17	40	0	0	6	24	11	73	9	47	7	30
Whether Her Education Was Needed for Job												
1. very much or somewhat	34	81	2	100	23	92	9	60	15	79	19	83
2. hardly or not at all	8	19	0	0	2	8	6	40	4	21	4	17

what she has learned is also involved in this question. Respondents incorporated both interpretations into their answers.   Future studies might profitably treat this subject
in greater depth than was possible here.   On-site observation of various work situations would prove useful.

Most respondents answer in very general terms when
asked what they like or dislike most about work.   The largest number (about one-third) say that they like teaching or
teaching a particular subject, while almost 30 per cent mentioned contact with students or clients.   Interaction with
those they serve evidently provides more satisfaction than
interaction with colleagues.   Only a few women mention
specific parts of their jobs--such as doing library work or
writing reports--that are found enjoyable.   Some would say
no more than that they like everything about their work, and
probing did not elicit more information.

In describing what they like least about their work,
respondents stress factors other than contact with students
or clients--even though "student indiscipline" is occasionally
mentioned.   Doing paper work of various sorts is the most
disliked activity, and is frequently described as routine or
uninteresting.   Teachers are required to do much correcting
of students' written work.   Clerks in government offices
may perform routine computations or mathematical work.
Inconvenience of working place or times is mentioned again
as a disliked aspect of work.   A number of individuals insist that there is nothing that they dislike about their work.
As has been suggested earlier, respondents are evidently
reluctant to criticize their jobs.   It may be, too, that "liking one's job" is not an important value and that other criteria such as the job's importance or the security provided
by it are weighed much more heavily.

Few individuals evidence a thoughtful approach to, or
examination of, the work they are doing, nor do they provid
much detail about their actual duties.   As noted in Chapter
IV, their desire to work is not usually based upon interest
in the intrinsic nature of a particular job.

Shils' observations about the approach of Indian intel-
lectuals to their work are relevant here.   He asserts that
Indians in intellectual professions are characterized by "vocational apathy."[21]   Shils partially accounts for this by the
explanation that professions are imposed on individuals rath-
than chosen freely, but also relates this stance to the mini-

mization of wordly preoccupations in Indian culture. His
generalizations are probably even truer for women, since
work is more often thought of as a way of filling time or
supplementing family income than as a focus of personal
involvement.   This vocational apathy may lessen as women
become more interested in their work or see it as a way of
contributing to the nation.   That critical interest in one's
own field and in teaching methods can gradually grow is illustrated in this tale of her own development told by a young
Brahmin college instructor:

> The subjects are not taught in an interesting way.
> I only became interested in zoology after taking
> my M. Sc.   My father wanted me to get married
> right after my B. Sc., but I didn't want, so I took
> up the M. Sc.   But I was not interested in the sub-
> ject.   I only went to college to have good times,
> and many of us did.   I had no thought of continuing
> so I thought, "If I get third class, it's good
> enough. " I thought that I would never use my
> education.   I was lucky enough to get a second
> class, so I got a place and could go on....
> We have to teach in a way that is not interest-
> ing to the students and not interesting to us.   We
> should be able to teach generally first and com-
> paratively.   Instead we go into each part in a
> given order.   There is a lot to cover, and that
> means in the third year everything is piled up....
> The older people don't want to change the curri-
> culum, but some of them are beginning to see the
> need for change.

A great devotion to task is perhaps more natural
when it is tied in with a sense of religious mission.   A
young Christian woman of the Pentecostal church, who has
not been included in the working sample because her efforts
are voluntary, might be quoted here:

> I have chosen throughout my life to do social serv-
> ice and religious work, helping the poor and needy,
> advising the ignorant for a better and peaceful life,
> showing them the right way to hate evil habits and
> turn their minds towards God and to their daily
> duties.

Since this woman has rejected marriage as a goal, she finds
no conflict between her religious efforts and other roles.   Her

remarks that she would marry if fate turned up a man with similar dedication sounded strangely similar to those made by women who said they would be willing to marry if it did not interrupt their education!

Working respondents were asked what jobs they migh prefer to their present ones. While more than a third clai to be content with their own jobs, the most frequent alterna tive, named by about one-fifth, is work in a bank. Jobs in banks are considered "fashionable"--glamorous, remunera- tive and the newest kind of work permitted to their daughte by some middle-class families. "Research," which usually refers to work towards a Ph. D., is the next most frequent choice. Candidates for Ph. D. 's are paid a stipend, enablin the individual to earn as well as attain her doctorate. The early interest in medicine expressed by seven women at some point in their interviews, was not mentioned as an alternate career choice. Women answered this question in terms of other positions for which they felt qualified rather than in terms of their previous aspirations. Three of the respondents' mothers, as compared to two respondents, are or have been physicians; these figures suggest that medicine has a history of acceptability as a field for women.

Attitudes about specific jobs, based on responses to this question and others, can be summarized in this way: While clerical jobs are still not considered totally satisfac- tory, those in banks are considered most prestigious and exciting. Teaching continues to be considered the most ac- ceptable and respectable work for women, and college lec- turers enjoy considerable prestige. Only a lucky few wome end up in medicine, despite the fact that it is an early aspi ration for many more of them. Research for a Ph. D. has a double advantage in that it satisfies the desire to continue one's education and at the same time brings in a stipend. At least for the present, respondents seen resigned to work in the few fields now open to them.

Notes

1. International Labour Review, "Women in the Labour Force," 77 (March 1958): no. 3, pp. 254-272.

2. The National Institute of Social Sciences.

3. Hans Nagpaul considers problematic the fact that in

India "social work has always been understood to be synonymous with voluntary service. " From "Dilemmas of Social Work Education in India, " Indian Journal of Social Work, 28 (October 1967): no. 3, p. 269. Respondents refer to social work in this way. K. V. Sridharan, Director of the National Institute of Social Sciences has mentioned in a private communication that many of the well-known schools of social work in India were started by voluntary social workers.

4. According to Dr. Sridharan, graduates of his school frequently seek employment in government factories and industries. The latter provide a number of social services and frequently include housing quarters.

5. This small sample of paid female workers may be considered indicative of the prevailing rates in Bangalore at the time of the study, since salaries for particular jobs are fairly standardized. The respondent working in the United States as a teaching assistant is omitted from Table 22 and certain other tables.

6. Dichotomizing income above and below 200 rupees per month, the difference in salary between teachers and clerks is not statistically significant for this group. The figures given represent teaching salaries. Income may be somewhat underrepresented, as teachers often take private pupils for tutoring ("tuitions") to supplement their incomes. Students doing post graduate work may also take pupils, and one clerk indicated that she was doing so.

7. Salary was a rather neutral question to us, but not to our Indian assistants. They sometimes asked further questions if a reported salary seemed unusually out of line. Respondents themselves sometimes found it necessary to explain how their salaries happened to be so low, adding, for example, "this salary is only temporary as I am expecting an increase soon. "

8. The bachelor of law is frequently taken with the notion of qualifying for higher positions rather than practicing law.

9. Research refers to doing research towards the Ph. D.

10.   The practice of having hot lunches delivered from home
      persists even in the cosmopolitan city of Bombay,
      where the massive problem of distributing some
      lunches to thousands of workers, and later picking
      up empty lunch containers, has not proven insoluable.
      These containers must be picked up, for the preju-
      dice against carrying things is still strong in the
      middle class.

11.   Much of what has been said about meals applies only
      to the middle and upper classes. Perhaps one of
      the distinctions made between classes in the city
      is based on whether or not members have the right
      to take specific time off for meals. Servants gen-
      erally eat well after others have eaten, and drivers
      may be on duty for hours without a real break for
      meals. Some change is taking place, however.
      Some of the postgraduates of our acquaintance are
      permitted to have coffee or a snack at three or four
      places in Bangalore. The university had newly re-
      furbished its canteen (snack shop) and encouraged
      women students to patronize it--somewhat success-
      fully.

12.   As in other societies, medicine appears to be the one
      profession the prestige of which can compete with
      the marriage role. While a number of respondents
      feel that an unmarried physician can lead a happy
      and worthwhile life, this need not be taken to mean
      that women physicians are difficult to marry off.
      The marriage of male and female physicians appears
      to be a preferred combination, wherein work and
      home roles can be made to complement each other.
      Thus, marriage to a male physician can enhance the
      woman physician's value rather than creating prob-
      lems of role conflict. In a somewhat different way,
      a woman who is a university lecturer will have both
      prestige and a relatively good salary to offer her
      future mate, and such jobs are eagerly sought.

13.   In suggesting the reform of existing scales of teachers'
      salaries in higher secondary schools, the Education
      Commission still proposes "advance increments" for
      teachers with first and second class in B. A. /B. Sc.
      or M. A. /M. Sc.   Report of the Education Commission
      Education and National Development (New Delhi:
      Government of India Press, 1968), p. 55.   That is,

those teachers having first or second class degrees would receive higher salaries than those who have third class.   On the other hand, M. A. 's with third class have been known to obtain teaching posts in colleges.   Here other influences come to bear--for example, the preference for a Christian teacher by a Christian college.

14.   The dearth of typewriters apparent to the western eye is obviously an illusion; typewriters must be in use more widely if this skill is in demand.

15.   What is here represented as religious prejudice might be considered a variant of casteism.   Being specifically a Moslem is not as important, for some purposes, as being a nonmember of a highly influential caste.

16.   Sengupta maintains that men are usually chosen over women as social workers in government factories, despite the presence of many women workers who would presumably welcome a woman's assistance. Padmini Sengupta, Women Workers of India (Bombay: Asia Publishing House, 1960), p. 83.   The Education Commission Report stresses the need for women teachers.   Op. cit. , pp. 63-64.

17.   Rosen shows a 28. 5 per cent increase in educated unemployed from the early 1950's to 1961, from 200, 000 in 1955 to 1, 000, 000 in 1961.   George Rosen, Democracy and Economic Change in India (Berkeley: University of California Press, 1966), table 21, p. 178.

18.   Chi-square = 7. 029, d. f. = 1, which is significant at . 01.

19.   Chi-square = 11. 004, d. f. = 1, which is significant at . 01.

20.   Chi-square = 5. 893, d. f. = 1, which is significant at . 05.

21.   Edward Shils, The Intellectual Between Tradition and Modernity: The Indian Situation (The Hague: Mouton and Co. , 1961), pp. 25-26.

Chapter VII

CONCLUSION

The position of women has varied throughout India's vast history. [1] Invasion and conquest, interpretations and re-interpretations of sacred writings, the joint family system and the economics of marriage have all played a part in bringing Indian women to that state of formal and legal subservience condemned by Mahatma Gandhi, Raja Ram Mohan Roy, Annie Besant and other great reformers of this century.

Child marriage had become obligatory by the beginning of the Christian era, in order to prevent the vulnerable sex from falling into evil ways. By the 19th century, the low level of literacy found in India especially characterized its women. Not only was widow remarriage forbidden, but in some regions the practice of sati was viewed as the most noble demonstration of wifely loyalty. Women were considered to be dependent on men for life: first their fathers, then husbands, then sons. Those who accepted this definition of themselves most fully were idealized and respected for their uncomplaining devotion as wives and mothers. Some were able to develop significant influence within their formally inferior roles, undoubtedly as a product of their artful sensitivity to the needs and whims of men. Thus, informal power was sometimes achieved, especially by the older women who ruled over domestic life. The lot of the new bride was frequently especially hard.

Then came the Independence Movement when, for the sake of the nation, and in line with their characteristic selflessness, Indian women forsook their homes to join in public demonstrations and to share the risk of arrest and imprisonment. Since Independence, elevating the position of women has become a major national goal. Even though national goals do not constitute current reality, the central government has been able to speed change by instituting legislative reforms and providing educational and economic advantages to women. Well-known leaders have added ideological support to counter

traditional prejudices. Plans for economic development and
population control consciously take into consideration the need
to raise women's status.

The 97 women in our sample represent a group most
subject to changing definitions of the female role. They are
urban, highly educated, and middle class. Many of them
work, or will work. They have more contact with the world
beyond the home than their less-educated middle class sisters. In a sample which included Hindus from various communities, Moslems, and Christians, we found many of their
concerns and life conditions to be similar. Despite the anti-
Brahmin movement in the South, this sample, taken from all
women graduates and postgraduates of Bangalore University
in 1965, was 53 per cent Brahmin. Thus, the long tradition
of education within Brahmin families, and the advantages con-
ferred by early socialization to it, as well as previously privileged position helps to keep this caste overrepresented
among successful students.

The women interviewed value college attendance as a
highly desirable experience, one to be extended as long as
possible and to be recommended to others. Among urban
families already convinced of the importance of education
for their sons, "putting" daughters in college becomes convenient and necessary. Faced with an older marriage age,
the increased availability of college education, and the delays
involved in arranging marriages, parents accept the opportunity to keep their daughters busy in a worthwhile way.
Traditional notions about women's sexuality are involved in
the wish to keep them fully occupied. Too, parents can be
less anxious about finding a bridegroom if their daughter is
not merely sitting at home awaiting their success in marriage arrangements.

But college education has certain unintended consequences. It creates in young women the desire to extend
this period of relative freedom from responsibility through
further education or "taking up" a job. The rising cost of
living, of educating many children, and sometimes of providing dowry, appears to have counterbalanced traditional
pressures against allowing middle class daughters to work.
Besides, the graduate woman can qualify for certain respectable jobs. Though new employment opportunities are
opening, not all of these are considered "suitable"; the
working women in the sample are employed only as lecturers, teachers, clerks and doctors. If new types of work

are compensated well in salary and prestige, they may grad
ally be added to the list of suitable jobs.

Another writer has observed that young Indian women
lack interest in the subjects they study. [2] In this they differ
little from many Indian men.   Fields of study are ranked in
prestige, and getting into the best profession for which one
can qualify takes precedence over the young person's own
interests.   Thus, as Shils has shown, many Indian intellec-
tuals are in fields that were chosen for them rather than by
them. [3]   Part of the lack of interest in education may be attributed to outmoded teaching methods and an emphasis on
examinations.   Even so, college attendance is so positive an
experience in other ways that many young women hope to
continue.   It provides the opportunity for a freedom of move
ment that they have not had before and are not likely to experience again, unless they become employed.   Less than
30 per cent of the sample expect to end their education with
a bachelor's degree.

The meshing of the marriage system with education
and employment creates potentials for change.   A college de
gree is viewed as an asset in the marriage market more
often than is employment.   However, under the arranged
marriage system, the more education a woman receives the
more highly educated a husband she will require.   For this
kind of husband, the cost of dowry frequently becomes pro-
hibitive.   If a woman has acquired her first degree, and a
mate is not found, a face saving alternative is to permit he
to continue her education.   Her requirements for a husband
become even more difficult to meet and her own assets may
be declining.   Perhaps in anticipation of the possibility that
they may have been educated out of the marriage market,
many of the respondents maintain that a woman can be happy
without marriage.   They point to the other alternatives she
now has which will keep her occupied.   Living arrangements
continue to be difficult for unmarried women.   Those who
see no satisfactory alternative to marriage point to the fact
that after her parents' death, the spinster will have to live
with a brother and sister-in-law.   None of the respondents
question women's dependence on male relatives as chaperone
throughout their live.   This is, perhaps, one of the assumptions that Western women will find most difficult to understand.

Employment is viewed as less advantageous in its ef
fects on marriage, as women recognize the continuing pres-

sures against those who work.   On the other hand, they are
aware of the opportunity to help their future husbands financially and the increasing role an employed woman can play
in choosing her mate.   Because they associate with men and
are better able to form judgments about them, working wom-
en may feel freer to exercise their right to veto their parent's choice.   A small number of respondents even say that
an employed woman can choose her own husband.   It is possible that, in the future, some families may weigh a prospective bride's earning capacity against their need for dowry.

The positive view of education is applied to its role
in marital adjustments.   Most women believe that their
broader experiences will make them more tolerant in relating to in-laws, rather than make them too independent.
Those who are married explicitly describe their attempts to
cater to less-educated in-laws, in order to show that their
education has not "ruined" them.

The employment problems found most pressing by this
sample of educated women are the lack of available jobs
suited to their educational attainments, the role of factors
such as influence and the need for special kinds of degrees
or skills to obtain jobs, and the relatively high level of unemployment, even for college graduates.   Their concerns focus on the problems of the educated in general, rather than
those of their own sex.   But underlying many remarks is the
assumption that restrictions on the movements of women, and
the convenience of working place and time, are important
considerations.   The working woman may not be permitted
to take up residence away from the parental home and, if
she does, her living conditions must be carefully arranged.
Because of economic necessity, the woman worker is allowed
to travel to and from her job, but she continues to be restricted in her social life.   While many employed women continue to rely on male relatives for chaperonage on their days
off, the accompaniment of female friends and relatives is beginning to be an acceptable substitute.   The practice of "dating" is certainly not condoned in Bangalore, although it sometimes occurs surreptitiously.   Certainly it would be helpful to
examine the social life of unmarried females in such cities
as Bombay or New Delhi in order to anticipate trends toward
possible breakdown of the restrictions observed.

These college educated women voice a preference for
jobs as lecturers, bank clerks, or research workers; most
of the working women in the sample are teachers.   Medicine

is a youthful aspiration for some, but social work or nursing
are notably absent as occupational choices.   Social work is
still thought of as a charitable avocation.   Women who work
give much of their salary to their families.   This economic
role, while new, fits in with more traditional expectations
that daughters will be of service to the family and that incomes will be pooled.

As their economic role is recognized, some working
women will be freed, voluntarily or involuntarily, from the
requirement that they marry.   We encountered nine women
who insist that they neither wish nor intend to marry.   For
some this is a way of freeing parents from the obligations
of mate selection and dowry; for others it is a protest
against the arranged marriage system.   But most respondents expect their parents to choose husbands for them and
to be given a chance to approve the choice.   These young
women hope to avoid any open splits with their families or
actions that might hurt their parents.   None see any alternative for the unmarried female but to accept the practice
of chaperonage and the need to eventually live with brothers.
They recognize the marriage state and motherhood as the
prime status through which women gain recognition--and
where in the world is it otherwise?   At the same time their
desire to work is partially prompted by the wish to be "independent, " to have some income and individuality of their
own.

                    *   *   *

The educated girl knows how to behave but she has
some independence of mind.   She doesn't have to
be a doormat.   She can think for herself and doesn't
have to agree to everything.   [A Christian.]

The trouble is that many [girls] will get their education and then stay at home.   There is still the
feeling that work is below their dignity.   I don't
feel that way.   They think they won't get good hus
bands if they work.   Women still have that sense
of subordination to men.   They feel it is their
duty.   They sit at home and wait to be married...
I think we must feel equal.   And with equality
comes responsibility.   We must do away with that
inferiority....   In five or ten years all will be
working.   Because financial difficulties are such
now.   It is very hard for everyone.   The boys

even now want their wives to be earning.   [A non-
Brahmin Hindu.]

If you ask many girls whether they prefer to live
or die, they will say die.   They feel there is nothing for them, the government hasn't provided.
We feel it would be better to be upper class or
lower class.   The middle class girls can't move
as freely.   If a girl is lower class, no one will
say anything if she goes out to work.   An upper
class girl also can do what she wants.   But it is
hardest in the middle class.   People will always
use their tongues and criticize.   There are many
restrictions.   [A non-Brahmin Hindu.]

I have a friend whom I want to marry.   He is doing
an M. Sc.   In fact, he's doing it because I'm doing
my M. A.   My mother is against it....   He's sort
of from a lower caste.   My mother considers ours
to be a "big family, " better than others.   We're
Christians, but from a high caste group.   This
boy's aunt once worked as a servant, so Mommy
says they're from a lower group.   And he's a little dark.   Mother's always worrying about color.
She'll tell us to put a little powder on when we go
out....   I went to the movies with him last week
and I told her, and there was quite a lot of trouble
about it.   She calls me a slut and says I am ruin-
ing things for my sister.   [A Christian.]

I think the highly educated woman in India still
isn't treated right.   She can't do what she would
like to do.   Opportunities are limited so she must
take what is offered, not what she likes.   Even
when she is employed, it is not easy.   There may
be difficulty with colleagues.   Each has his own
ideas and won't adjust to other people's point of
view.   There is too much of superiority.   The
older people won't listen to the views of the
younger people.   They won't consider our ideas,
what we think.   [A Brahmin.]

Proper opportunities must be given to educated
women, for employment and for those who are
interested in higher studies....   They say we
should only want to serve, but the money is needed,
too, these days for the standard of living.   So

> how can we not care about that too? Then people
> ask how much we earn and they say, 'What, so
> little with an M. A. ?' [A Moslem]

The foregoing comments are not typical. They represent the views of some of the more outspoken women we
met.   These are the ones who are willing to express dissatisfaction, who see the need for change.   Education has
not brought them the kind of opportunities or rights to which
they feel entitled.   Much of their concern about jobs reflects
the general problems of the educated unemployed.   The alternative to unemployment is take a job that is beneath one's
qualifications, something which is hard for an Indian to do.
Some young women deplore both the continuing social pressures that circumscribe their movements and also the members of their own sex who uncritically accept an image of
inferiority and subordination.   Education and employment are
beginning to be viewed as mechanisms which will lead to
greater independence and more equality.

The picture observed is one of gradual change, but of
change that was not easily foreseen a few decades ago.   It
has been suggested that certain traditional beliefs and practices facilitated some of these developments.   Women whom
the author met while in India are now engaged in occupations
that their parents would have forbidden a few years ago.

These changes carry within them the potential for
further ones.   As Musgrove points out, "New institutions
may be accepted because they seem to lend support to existing social values; but their long term effect may be to under
mine them. "[4] Middle class parents who now see college edu
cation as a natural and even necessary attainment for their
daughters cannot control all the consequences that follow.
One of the most significant of these is the economic independ
ence gained by the educated employed daughter.   Although the
educated woman still professes concern and respect for the
wishes of her parents and future in-laws, she is gradually
gaining in status within the family.

Young Indian women as a group have held a very low
position in their families and in their society, regardless of
the affection with which they may have been regarded.   It is
not surprising then that they so eagerly embrace the opportunity that college-going provides.   They need not be interested in a particular subject in order to enjoy the freedom
and fellowship of their peers that they experience away from

home.   They need not really care for the content of their
studies in order to appreciate the enhanced status that a college degree brings.   They need not like a particular job in
order to derive satisfaction from earning their own money.
At the same time, the new freedoms and opportunities are
still combined with old restrictions and with traditional notions about women's dependence on male protection.   The educated woman will have views not shared by her mother or
mother-in-law; and some of these views will be supported by
scientific knowledge she has learned at school.

The employed woman acts both in the status of an
educated person who can "mix with" men and women of different castes and religions and, at home, as an obedient,
subservient and somewhat ignorant young female.   The possibility of role conflict is growing.   Musgrove points out that
it was middle and upper class British women of the late Vic-
torian and Edwardian England whose status frustrations led
to the militant Suffragette movement. [5]   While we have not,
in this book, attempted a comparative review of the women's
movement in various countries, nor its preconditions, it is
obvious that the story of Indian women belongs in such a
comparative study.

It should also be reiterated that this book represents
a first attempt to study women who have recently graduated
from Indian universities, in a personal interview situation. [6]
Just as a number of studies have now been done on women
college students, it will be important to add others which
follow the educated Indian woman through various stages in
her life cycle.

Notes

1.   See for example, P. Thomas, Indian Women Through the
      Ages, (Bombay: Asia Publishing House, 1964); K.
      M. Kapadia, Marriage and Family in India, 3rd ed.
      rev. (Bombay: Oxford University Press, 1966),
      chapter 11; and A. S. Altekar, The Position of Wom-
      en in Hindu Civilization, 3rd ed. (Delhi: Motilal
      Banarsidass, 1962).

2.   Aileen D. Ross, Student Unrest in India (Montreal: Mc-
      Gill-Queen's University Press, 1969).

3.   Edward Shils, The Intellectual Between Tradition and

Modernity (The Hague: Mouton and Co. , 1961), pp.
25-26.

4.   F. Musgrove, Youth and the Social Order (Bloomington:
      Indiana University Press, 1965), p. 130.

5.   Ibid. , p. 126.

6.   Rama Mehta's study of an older generation of educated
      women was published after this manuscript had been
      drafted, and was not available during the course of
      this research.   Her book is valuable in presenting
      the views of an older, elite group of college-educated
      married women.

Appendix

INTERVIEW SCHEDULE

Sociology Department
Bangalore University

Dear Graduate and Post-Graduate:
May we ask your assistance in this research on the
role of the woman graduate and post-graduate in
Bangalore? It is being done under the guidance of
the Sociology Department, Bangalore University.
The questionnaire deals with both opportunities and
problems of highly educated women. A sample of
women has been selected from a list of graduates
and post-graduates, and you are one of those selected.
Please be frank in answering these questions. All
information will be kept confidential. It will be
used only to obtain a general picture of the opportunities and problems of graduate and post-graduate
women. Your signature is not required. But please
feel free to add your own comments in answering.
Thank you very much for your assistance.

Sincerely yours,

Dr. (Mrs.) Rhoda L. Goldstein
Fulbright Research Scholar
Bangalore University

I. EDUCATION

1. Please tick off the institution(s) attended, giving degrees obtained and date of graduation:

	Degree	Date
___Acharya Pathasala	_____	_____
___Bangalore Medical College	_____	_____
___Central College	_____	_____

157

<table>
<tr><td>____Home Science</td><td>_____</td><td>_____</td></tr>
<tr><td>____Law College</td><td>_____</td><td>_____</td></tr>
<tr><td>____Maharani's College</td><td>_____</td><td>_____</td></tr>
<tr><td>____Malleswaram Education Society</td><td>_____</td><td>_____</td></tr>
<tr><td>____M. E. S. College</td><td>_____</td><td>_____</td></tr>
<tr><td>____Mount Carmel College</td><td>_____</td><td>_____</td></tr>
<tr><td>____National College</td><td>_____</td><td>_____</td></tr>
<tr><td>____Rashtreeya Vidyalaya</td><td>_____</td><td>_____</td></tr>
<tr><td>____Teachers College</td><td></td><td></td></tr>
<tr><td>___Vijaya College</td><td>_____</td><td>_____</td></tr>
</table>

2. Major subjects studied _____

3. What other subject or field did you consider majoring in? (If another subject was considered, how is it that you did not major in this field?)

II. PRESENT ACTIVITIES

1. Are you at present:
   __married __widowed __unmarried __separated
      If married: If unmarried:
   a. Husband's education: a. Are you engaged?
                              ___yes ___no
   b. Husband's occupation: b. If engaged, about when do you expect to be married?
   c. With regard to living arrangements are you living: c. If engaged, please give future husband's education:
      ___independently
      ___with husband's family   d. If engaged, please give future husband's occupation:
      ___other (explain)

2. Is it the custom to accept dowry in your community?
   ___yes ___no. Other (explain):

3. Are you at present: (Please tick off answer that applies to you)
   ___doing post-graduate studies? (Give institution and major subject.)
   ___planning to do further studies? (Please explain.)
   ___not now planning to do any further studies.

4. Please explain which family members have most strongly influenced decisions about your education.

158

5. How do the above family members feel about a girl attending a co-educational college?

6. Are you at present:

___employed outside home   ___not employed; not seeking employment
___not employed; seeking employment   ___not seeking employment; would like to work

7. Suppose your family was very well off and there were no financial difficulties whatsoever, would you: ___prefer to work; ___prefer not to work. Please explain why:

8. IF YOU ARE NOW EMPLOYED, please indicate how family members feel about your working. IF YOU ARE NOT NOW EMPLOYED, indicate how family members feel about your seeking employment:

Father	Mother
___strongly encourages	___strongly encourages
___mildly encourages	___mildly encourages
___doesn't mind	___doesn't mind
___minds somewhat	___minds somewhat
___prefers I stay home	___prefers I stay home
___other (specify):	___(other (please specify):

Brother 1 (eldest)	Brother 2
___strongly encourages	___strongly encourages
___mildly encourages	___mildly encourages
___minds somewhat	___minds somewhat
___prefers I stay home	___prefers I stay home
___other (specify):	___other (please specify):

Brother 3	Sister(s)
___strongly encourages	___strongly encourages
___mildly encourages	___mildly encourages
___minds somewhat	___minds somewhat
___prefers I stay home	___prefers I stay home
___other (specify):	___other (please specify):

Husband/husband-to-be

___strongly encourages   Describe feeling of
___mildly encourages   other influential family
___doesn't mind   members not mentioned
___minds somewhat   above:
___prefers I stay home
___other (please specify):

9. This question deals with activities other than work. Last week, about how many hours did you spend in the following activities? Please fill in the number of hours before each activity:

a___ studying and attending classes or lectures

b___ assisting in the household

c___ visiting with friends at your home or theirs

d___ reading for enjoyment

e___ listening to music at home

f___ engaging in sports

g___ going to a restaurant, hotel or club

h___ going to the cinema

i___ visiting with family members at your home or theirs

j___ applying for jobs

k___ applying for schools or scholarships

l___ engaging in a type of learning at home. (Please specify what) and number of hours:

m___ Please add any other major activities and time spent.

10. Do you find that you are busy:
___ all of the time
___ most of the time
___ some of the time
___ not at all busy

III. FOR THOSE NOW EMPLOYED

Please answer the questions below if you are now employed.

1. Please describe your position and actual work as fully as possible. For example, if you are a teacher, name school and standard taught. Position is:
___ temporary or
___ permanent.

2. What are your hours of work? From _____ to _____.

3. Your salary? _____ per _____.

4. How long have you held this position?
____ years ____ months

III. FOR THOSE NOT NOW EMPLOYED

Please answer the questions below if you are not now employed.

1. Have you applied for any jobs? ___yes ___no (If yes, what was the result?)

2. Have you been employed since graduation? ___yes ___no. (If yes, please describe your last position and actual work.)

3. How long did you remain in this job?
____ under 3 months
____ 3-5 months
____ 6-12 months
____ more than 1 year

160

5. Did your education prepare you for your present
   work?
   ___very much so
   ___somewhat
   ___hardly at all
   ___my education was not
   needed for this job
6. Do you find your work is:
   ___very interesting
   ___somewhat interesting
   ___not at all interesting
7. Do you find your work is:
   ___very tiring
   ___somewhat tiring
   ___not at all tiring
8. What do you like most
   about your present work?
9. What do you like least
   about your present work?
10. In what way are the hours
    and place of work con-
    venient or inconvenient
    for you?
11. How much financial assist-
    ance are you contributing
    to your family per month?
    If married, how much fi-
    nancial assistance are you
    contributing to your hus-
    band's family per month?
12. How much do you keep for
    personal expenses per
    month?
13. Did you work at any other
    position before taking this
    one? ___yes ___no
    If yes, for how long?
    ___years ___months.
    If yes, please describe the
    position and actual work.
    What was the reason for
    changing jobs?
14. What other job, if any,
    would you have preferred
    to your present position?
15. Which family members
    have most strongly influ-
    enced decisions about
    your working?

4. What was the reason for
   leaving the position?
5. What did you like most
   about that job?
6. What did you like least
   about that job?

If you have held more than
one job since graduation,
please add the same in-
formation about the pre-
vious job.

PLEASE TURN TO QUES-
TION IV ON THE NEXT
PAGE.

161

IV. FOR ALL GRADUATES AND POST-GRADUATES

We would like to have your <u>personal</u> opinion on problems of the educated woman. Please remember that this information is confidential, so be frank.

1. Judging from the experiences of your friends and yourself, what would you say are the main problems of the woman graduate in Bangalore?
   a. With regard to employment.
   b. With regard to the finding of a suitable partner.
      Do you think that <u>education</u> helps or hinders a girl in finding a suitable partner? Please explain. Do you think that <u>being employed</u> helps or hinders a girl in finding a suitable partner? Please explain.
   c. Problems in marriage. What do you think are the major adjustments an educated woman will have to make in marriage?
      Do you think that education helps or hinders her in making these adjustments?
      At about what age do you think a girl should get married?

2. Under what conditions, if any, do you feel that a married woman without children should work outside the home?

3. Under what conditions, if any, should a mother work outside the home?

4. Do you think that a girl who does not marry can lead a happy life or that she cannot? Please explain.

5. Do you feel you are expected to contribute to the society in any special ways because of your education? Please explain.

6. If a friend's younger sister came to you for advice about going to college, what would you say to her?

7. If you could do anything you wanted to in the next two years, what would you choose to do?

V. STATISTICAL DATA

Please add the following data about yourself; do not sign your name.

_____ age	_____ no. of brothers
_____ religion	Their education:
_____ caste	_____ no. of sisters
_____ sub-caste	Their education:
_____ father's job	
_____ father's education	
_____ mother's job, if any	
_____ mother's education	

Please tick off which of the following family members are now living in the same household as you:

___mother ___father ___grandparent(s) ___brother(s)
___sister(s) ___uncle(s) ___aunt(s) ___cousin(s)
___mother-in-law ___father-in-law ___brother(s)-in-law
___sister(s)-in-law

Please tick off approximate household income per month:
___below Rs. 150
___between 150-299
___between 300-499
___between 500-799
___above Rs. 800

What class do you consider your family to be?
___upper class
___upper middle class
___middle class
___lower middle class
___lower class
___other (what?)

THANK YOU VERY MUCH FOR YOUR CO-OPERATION.
PLEASE ADD ANY ADDITIONAL COMMENTS YOU WISH TO
MAKE ABOUT THE PROBLEMS AND OPPORTUNITIES OF
EDUCATED WOMEN IN BANGALORE.

Bibliography

Agarwala, B. R. "Review of The Hindu Family in Its Urban
    Setting, by Aileen D. Ross." Sociological Bulletin 12
    (1963): 75-78.
Altekar, A. S. The Position of Women in Hindu Civilization.
    3rd edition, Delhi: Motilal Banarsidass, 1962.
American Academy of Political and Social Science. "Women
    Around the World," The Annals 375 (January 1968).
Anand, Kulwant. "Attitudes of Punjab University Women
    Students Toward Marriage and the Family," Indian Journal
    of Social Work 26 (1965): 87-90.
Aneja, Nirmala. "Use of Higher Education by Women,"
    Social Welfare 13 (September 1966): 1-3.
Bagal, Jogesh Chandra. Women's Education in Eastern India
    the First Phase. Calcutta: The World Press Private
    Limited, 1956.
Bangalore University. Convocation; Monday, the 6th De-
    cember 1965. Document of Bangalore University, March
    12, 1965.
Barnabas, A. P. and Mehta, Subhash C. Caste in Changing
    India. New Delhi: Indian Institute of Public Administra-
    tion, 1965.
Basham, A. L. "Indian Society and the Legacy of the Past,"
    Australian Journal of Politics and History 12 (1966): 131-
    145.
Besant, Annie. Wake Up, India: A Plea for Social Reform.
    Adyar, Madras: Theosophical Publishing House, 1913.
Béteille, André. Caste, Class and Power. Berkeley:
    University of California Press, 1965.
Bhatnagar, I. "Spinsters," Social Welfare 11 (April 1964):
    19.
Blood, Robert O., Jr. Love Match and Arranged Marriage.
    Glencoe, N. Y.: The Free Press, 1967.
Bondurant, Joan. "Traditional Polity and the Dynamics of
    Change in India," Human Organization 22 (Spring 1963):
    5-10.
Breese, Gerald. Urbanization in Newly Developing Societies.
    Englewood Cliffs, N. J.: Prentice-Hall, 1966.
Cormack, Margaret L. The Hindu Woman, originally pub-

lished by Teacher's College, Columbia University, 1953.
Bombay: Asia Publishing House edition, 1961.
_____. She Who Rides a Peacock. Bombay: Asia Pub-
lishing House, 1961.
Cousins, Margaret E. Indian Womanhood Today. Rev. ed.,
Allahabad: Kitabistan, 1947.
Datta, K. K. Renaissance, Nationalism and Social Changes
in Modern India. Calcutta: Bookland Private Limited,
1965.
Degler, Carl. "Revolution Without Ideology: The Changing
Place of Women in America," in The Woman in America,
edited by Robert Jay Lifton, pp. 192-210. Boston:
Beacon Press, 1964.
Dutt, G. S. A Woman in India (Life of Saroj Nalini).
London: Hogarth Press, 1929.
Felton, Monica. A Child Widow's Story. London: Victor
Gollancz, 1966.
Gandhi, M. K. Women and Social Injustice. Ahmedabad:
Navajivan Pub. House, 1942.
Ghurye, G. S. Caste and Race in India. 5th ed., rev.,
Bombay: Popular Prakashan, 1969.
Gist, Noel P. "Mate Selection and Mass Communication in
India," Public Opinion Quarterly (Winter 1953-54): 481-
495.
Goode, William J. World Revolution and Family Patterns.
London: Free Press of Glencoe, Collier-Macmillan, 1963.
Gusfield, Joseph R. "Tradition and Modernity: Misplaced
Polarities in the Study of Social Change," American Jour-
nal of Sociology 72 (January 1967): 351-362.
Hate, Chandrakala A. Hindu Woman and Her Future. Bom-
bay: New Book Co., 1948.
Hooja, Swarn. "Dowry System Among the Hindus in North
India: A Case Study," Indian Journal of Social Work 28
(January 1968): 411-426.
India (Republic) Ministry of Education. Report of the Edu-
cation Commission (1964-66). Education and National
Development ["Kothari Report"]. 1966.
India (Republic) Ministry of Information and Broadcasting,
Publications Division. The Gazeteer of India. Vol. 1,
"Country and People," 1965.
International Labour Review. "Women in the Labour Force."
Volume 77 (March 1968): 254-272.
Isaacs, Harold R. India's Ex-Untouchables. New York:
John Day, 1964.
Janeway, Elizabeth. Man's World, Woman's Place. New
York: William Morrow, 1971.
Kabir, Humayun. Education in New India. New York:

Harper and Brothers, 1955.

Kannan, C. T. Intercaste and Inter-Community Marriages in India. Bombay: Allied Publishers, Pvt., 1963.

Kapadia, K. M. "A Perspective Necessary for the Study of Social Change in India," Sociological Bulletin 6 (1957): 43-60.

———. Marriage and Family in India. 3rd ed., rev., Bombay: Oxford University Press, 1966.

Karve, Irawati. Kinship Organization in India. Deccan College Monograph Series, II. Poona, India: Deccan College Post-Graduate and Research Institute, 1953.

Keer, Dhananjay. Dr. Ambedkar: Life and Mission, 2nd ed., rev., Bombay: Popular Prakashan, 1962.

Khati, A. A. "Social Change in the Caste Hindu Family and its Possible Impact on Personality and Mental Health," Sociological Bulletin 12 (1963): 146-163.

Kurian, George. The Indian Family in Transition: A Case Study of Kerala Syrian Christians. The Hague: Mouton, 1961.

Lamb, Beatrice Pitney. India: A World in Transition, 2nd ed., rev., New York: Frederick Praeger, 1966.

Levy, Marion J., Jr. The Family Revolution in Modern China. Cambridge, Mass., Harvard University Press, 1949.

Lundberg, Ferdinand and Farnham, Marynia F. Modern Woman, The Lost Sex. New York: Harper and Brothers, 1947.

Mace, David and Mace, Vera. Marriage East and West. Garden City, N. Y.: Doubleday (Dolphin Book), 1959.

Mahajan, Amarjit. "Women's Two Roles: A Study of Role Conflict," Indian Journal of Social Work 26 (January 1966): 377-380.

Mandelbaum, David G. Society in India. 2 vols. Berkeley: University of California Press, 1970.

Mehta, Rama. The Western Educated Hindu Woman. New York: The Asia Pub. Co., 1970.

Menon, P. M. "Towards Equality of Opportunity in India," International Labour Review 94 (October 1966): 350-374.

Misra, B. B. The Indian Middle Classes; Their Growth in Modern Times. London: Oxford University Press, 1961.

Moore, Wilbert. "Predicting Discontinuities in Social Change," American Sociological Review 29 (1964): 331-338.

Musgrove, F. Youth and the Social Order. Bloomington: Indiana University Press, 1965.

Myrdal, Alva and Klein, Viola. Women's Two Roles: Home and Work. London: Routledge and Kegan Paul, 1956.

166

Nagpaul, Hans. "Dilemmas of Social Work Education in India," Indian Journal of Social Work 28 (October 1967): 269-284.

Nanavati, Manilal B. and Vakil, C. N., editors. Group Prejudices in India: A Symposium. Bombay: Vora and Co., 1951.

Papanek, Hanna. "The Woman Field Worker in a Purdah Society," Human Organization 23 (Summer 1964): 160-163.

Pimpley, P. N. and Anand, K. "Role of Occupation in Marital Alliances," Indian Journal of Social Work 25 (January 1965): 381-388.

Rao, G. R. S. "Emerging Role Patterns of Women in Family," Indian Journal of Social Work 26 (October 1965): 239-242.

Rosen, George. Democracy and Economic Change in India. Berkeley: University of California Press, 1965.

Ross, Aileen D. The Hindu Family in Its Urban Setting. Toronto: University of Toronto Press, 1961.

_____. Student Unrest in India; a Comparative Approach. Montreal: McGill-Queen's University Press, 1969.

Rudolph, Lloyd L. and Rudolph, Susanne. The Modernity of Tradition: Political Development in India. Chicago: University of Chicago Press, 1969.

Sengupta, Padmini. Women Workers of India. Bombay: Asia Publishing House, 1960.

Shastri, Shakuntala Rao. Women in the Sacred Laws. Bombay: Bharatiya Vidya Bhavan, 1959.

Shils, Edward. The Intellectual Between Tradition and Modernity: The Indian Situation. The Hague: Mouton, 1961.

Shrivedi, S. A Century of Indian Womanhood. Mysore: Rao and Raghavan, 1965.

Singh, Khushwant. "The Women of India," New York Times Magazine. March 13, 1966, p. 24+.

Social Welfare. "Spinsters," vol. 11 (April 1964): 19.

Sociological Bulletin. Symposium: Caste and Joint Family, vol. 4 (September 1955).

Srinivas, M. N. Marriage and Family in Mysore. Bombay: New Book Co. 1942.

Tampoc, Riva. "The Women of India," Contemporary Review 195 (January 1959): 23-26.

Theodorson, George A. "Cross-National Variations in Eagerness to Marry." In Comparative Perspectives on Marriage and the Family, edited by H. Kent Geiger. Boston: Little, Brown, 1968.

Thomas, P. Indian Women Through the Ages. Bombay: Asia Publishing House, 1964.

United Nations. Department of Economic and Social Affairs. The Mysore Population Study. A Co-operative project of the United Nations and the Government of India, Population Studies no. 34, 1961.

Venkatarayappa, K. N. Bangalore: A Socio-Ecological Study Bombay: University of Bombay Publications, 1957 (sociology series no. 6).

Verma, Malka, "Socio-Economic Study of Undergraduate Girl Students," Indian Journal of Social Work 21 (December 1960); 283-286.

Woodsmall, Ruth F. Women and the New East. Washington D. C. : The Middle East Institute, 1960.

169

DATE DUE			